Who Are You?

Written by:
Tim Evans

Copyright information:

Copyrights @ 2013 Tim Evans. Printed and bound in the United States of America. All rights reserved. No portion of this book may be reproduced or transmitted in any form or by any means, - electronic or mechanical, including photocopying, scanning, recording, or by any information storage and retrieval system – except for brief quotations in a critical reviews or articles without the prior written permission of the publisher.

Copyright office in accordance with title 17, United States Code, attest that registration has been made for the work identified as the title of work Who Are You? Author: Tim Evans, Author created: text, photographs. Copyright office registration number is TXu 1-864-417 effective date of registration: April 22, 2013

<u>*Information about the front cover:*</u>

This picture was taken at Trunk Bay, St. John Virgin Island. I took this image on a vacation in 2004. The image was selected to symbolize solitude that one needs to accomplish in identifying oneself. We need to evaluate ourselves in an individual personal manner. The calmness that is in our life in identifying ourselves of who we are is translated in this image. This image also represents how beautiful each person has potential in becoming. We each have an image that others will see a positive successful person in which they have become. When one looks at the cover I hope it gives a peace in you that can inspire each of us to be the person we each are intended to be. By always being truthful to our inner purpose we all will be able to identify our self and ask ourselves WHO ARE YOU?

Table of contents:

Copyright information...3

Information about the front cover 5

Dedication..9

Introduction...11

Chapter 1: Our society does not make us who we are...15

Chapter 2: Society's level of income and how it effects who you are..23

Chapter 3: Doing the right things no matter what others may think about us...41

Chapter 4: Relationships and how they affect who you are..55

Chapter 5: What identifies you as who you are?...75

Chapter 6: Remember where you came from and how it has developed who you have become..87

Chapter 7: Be happy with whom you are..*93*

Chapter 8: Inspirational thoughts written by me..*103*

Chapter 9: Good intentions..*109*

Chapter 10: Your purpose..*119*

Chapter 11: It is easier being who you are, than to be who other people want or think you should be..*129*

Chapter 12: Everyone has a story..*139*

Chapter 13: Only you are in control in identifying who you are..*149*

Chapter 14: Who are You?..*165*

Special thanks..*193*

Dedication:

I dedicate this book to my beautiful wife; for all that she does for everyone. I know we probably all cherish our spouse. I feel I have been truly blessed to have Cindy beside me through every aspect of my life. She supports me through everything and is the positive force in my life. Cindy is the rock of our family the one who holds everything together.  She is a great mom to both of our beautiful daughters. Lydia and Macey have been a great blessing in our lives. I have been so blessed to have such a great family. They help me to identify who I am. I love them dearly; they give me a purpose each day to do the best I can at everything. When I told Cindy that I was writing a book she never once expressed any negativity she just supported me. I am not surprised she supports me in everything. Anyone who knows anything about me would be shocked that I am writing a book, see I am a man with few words. I was inspired to write this book in hopes it might help others to identify who they are.

Introduction:

I have written this book to share some of my experiences and concepts with others; in hopes it may be encouraging to them. I have a great life that at times have its own challenges. I have found that it is how I respond to each of these challenges that identify me as an individual. I shared some of my experiences with a close friend, who expressed similar trials; this encouraged me to share with as many people as possible. We each have a unique story that can be inspirational to someone. In sharing myself with you, I hope this will spark a personal desire to explore yourself, and may inspire you to identify who you truly are. In society we are identified by different standards. You need to first identify who you are, and not who people think you are. You are the one who truly knows who you are for you know your thoughts and your intentions. We are faced with so many decisions every day that can impact how people identify you. It is important to know who you are and to feel good about whom you are. If you are not happy with yourself, do a self-evaluation; then take a moment to reflect on the things that need improving. We should not dwell on the things that we discover, but we should set goals for yourself. Be patient some goals may take longer to achieve. I know there are many ways I can improve myself. The way I acknowledge a lot of opportunities for improvement is by trial and error. It is important to learn from your error and try to grow from them, and not keep repeating the same mistakes. Try to surround yourself with positive thoughts and people.

     I am proud of the way my parents raised me. I believe that they applied their values into expectations, to be transpired into a personal action. My parent's expectation is for me to become successful within me, to set goals, and to achieve these goals, take pride in all that I do. I think you start from your childhood molding yourself of whom you are. That is not to say someone raised in bad situation that there is no hope, or someone from best situation is got it made and that they are the best person. We each are from a different background. It is important to realize we each must work at being who we are intended be, and to realize we each have a unique purpose. I think no matter what situation one may be faced with, as a child or adult it is how you handle each situation and learn from it that help mold you into who you are. I remember a molding experience; it was when I started school. It was not mandatory at that time for kids to go to kindergarten. My parents chose to start me in first grade instead of starting me in kindergarten. It was advised by the teachers to my parents to hold me back into first grade. This was devastating, for I thought I had failed first grade all through the years of my schooling. I felt as if I was not smart enough to pass the first grade, I built a low esteem all from this experience. It was not until I was an adult with a family that I realized I had not failed. My brother found all my old report cards and gave them to me. I looked at my grades from first grade and the grades were excellent. I now know I was not held back because of failing grades. Discovering this made the feeling of failure, (which I struggled with my entire life until that moment,) disappear. I had already completed my surgical technologist program before discovering this information. Finishing this program was a major accomplishment for me. I chose this career path reluctantly, for the thought of going back to school was a huge struggle for me. I believe we sometimes are able to surpass our own goals through our inner desire and dedication. This experience shows me that we each can surpass our own weakness, through applying oneself into the person we are to become.

Chapter 1: *Our society does not make us who we are.*

We are constantly being judged by society. It may be the way we dress, or the car we drive, house, or the neighborhood we live in. All these are materialistic and should have no influence on who you are. By our wonderful society it does. Sometimes opinions are formed before one is even given a chance. We live in an environment where the expectation of society is that everyone should be models living in a mansion. Reality is we are not all independently wealthy and drop dead gorgeous. Some people are fat while others are skinny, some are tall while others may be short, some are old and some are young. There are different ethnical groups. All the diversities that we encounter are not who a person is. It is what a person is made of, their experiences, and how they incorporate each decision that helps identify them as who they are. We should not treat others differently because the way they appear outwardly, for it is the inner person that truly counts and makes us the individuals that we all are. Everyone has a great potential of doing well, and we should treat people with the respect that they deserve. In life we are faced with much diversity, it is how we handle each of them that identify our strengths and weakness. So many times people look for any type of differences to validate their actions of treating someone in a poor manner. That does not give a person the authority to try to make someone who they are not; by simple appearance alone, and not who that person truly is. We are often stereotyped into someone else, instead of whom we are. I am just as guilty as the rest of the society, and I am sure that I have missed meeting some great people. In our day and time we all live such busy lives. It is how we treat others or take time for others that can make a positive impact on them.

  One of the doctors I know told me a story about his materialistic experience. He told me about his experience after I commented on liking his car. This doctor is very successful. Many years ago he drove a more common car and was content in driving it. This doctor was not materialistic driven; he only desired something reliable to drive. One day when he took the car in for routine service the mechanic replied to him doctor you drive this car you must not be very successful if that is all you can afford to drive. He had chosen to keep a low profile, however he realized that through this experience that materialistic items seem to characterize ones success. He now drives a nicer vehicle and indicates that the routine maintenance is extremely overpriced. He indicated his next car will be more practical and even more environmental friendly as well. His success is not measured by the car he drives but achieving his own personal goals. Many times I see people drive nice vehicles to impress others of a successful person instead of letting their success identify themselves as who they truly are. Society has images of success by the materialistic collection one claims as their own. What is it that you measure your success on?

Have you ever looked at a group photo of yourself with either friends or family? There are certain characteristics that separate you apart from others. These certain characteristics identify you as an individual by your physical appearance. We are limited to certain parameters to change our appearance, for our genes have the most influence on our appearance. We can dye our hair; change our hair styles, even put in color contact lenses to change our eye color. We can lose weight or gain weight that alters our appearance. We can have cosmetic surgery to alter or enhance certain things about you, however you will still be identified as who you are by the way people remember or identify you. Just the way people identify your appearance they also identify you by your inner self. People may perceive you as someone who is nice, or someone who is not. People *may identify many things about you. The one who is in full control or direct who you are is you. We are able to project ourselves as someone that always encourages others. We can be the person who truly cares about others. We can spend our time devoting and learning our intended path of success in our own desires of fulfilling our purpose in life. Our society may try to influence who you are, but you are to prove to everyone you and only you are in control of who you are. This path of inner desire is a path that surpasses any outer appearance it must be shared to others to be able to be identified as an individual. Once you have shared your inner self with others that will become your true identity of who you are. People will realize your intent or purpose in life by the way you live each day. We are constantly identifying ourselves as an individual not just by appearance, but by our actions of who we are.*

      Sometimes people will tend to try to develop into certain images that are not true to who they really are. They think by developing into these characteristics they will be more accepted. Instead it creates more challenges, financially and psychologically. Then people sometimes can feel trapped in a lifestyle that is very difficult or impossible to continue. Life is hard enough being who you are, but living a life that is not you at all must be even more difficult to just please others. Being who you are is more fun you do not have to worry about what others may think. Most likely by being yourself, you will be around other people with similar interest. I see people all time living a life that seems to be not true to them. It is important to live a life that makes you happy. Happiness is so important. There is nothing like being with family or friends that you can just laugh, not a fake laugh, but a deep belly laugh or maybe even a snort and no one even cares. Having self-inspired goals is a good thing since it is your goals for yourself, and not influenced by others. The basics in any relationship should start with who you are and who you develop into. We are constantly developing ourselves with each decision that we make, and how we react to each decision. Searching for who you are can be ongoing, and for some there is no searching at all. Society does not choose who you are, it may influence you, but who you are should be developed within, and not what others develop for you.

Growing up I was the youngest and I learned a lot by observing my brother and sister. They sometimes did things that got them into trouble with my parents. I would take a mental note and try not to duplicate the same results. I find a lot of my childhood memories have prepared me for my life lessons I experience today. Even as a child I would take note of certain behaviors and try to learn from other people's experiences. I believe these lessons have helped me mold into who I am today. I think it is how we react, even as a child to each decision that creates an impact on decisions that we are faced with in the future. I believe we are always building each decision to the next on who we are. Life is filled with so many lessons it is what you do with them that matters. Do we learn from them? Do we grow from them? I believe we should learn from them and grow from each experience. Every experience has a message. What we translate from these messages is how we are able to develop into a better person. I observed certain behaviors from my siblings as a child and noticed the results before it impacted my own life. I was learning from their experiences and applying it to my own life. We are never too young or too old to learn about ourselves in fulfilling our inner purpose.

      I often find myself getting caught up with my daily routine. Daily routine is a good habit as long as we are taking a moment to identify that we are on the right track of our inner self, and being successful in becoming who we are. Taking time off for vacation or a day here and there to reflect of who we truly are can be very beneficial. Time off can be refreshing from time to time it allows us to clear our mind of our monotonous routine, to rejuvenate ourselves into our intended purpose. The things that are important to us help us identify our inner self, and keep our goals in check. We should identify our purpose, and make sure the life we are living is in proper alignment in achieving these goals. I often find my daily routine to seem to be rushed up at times, and the things that should and would have mattered, are now lost on the way. We live in a competitive world and it seems to impact the things that truly matter. We should be able to reflect back on each day and be proud of each area of our life. There seems to always be an area in my reflection of where I should improve myself, in becoming that person that leaves a legacy for others to witness. I have my own goals to achieve, however, I hope my life can be a positive impact to the people I am around. This is important to me not to live a life to only please them, but my happiness that I have developed for myself may be shared by others around me. Willing to share our happiness and experiences with others identifies you as an individual; it will be strength for both you and others. We all can grow from our challenges, and be stronger to face them as they arise in the future. I once heard a saying "we are not stupid for making a mistake, what is stupid is repeating the same mistake over and over again." Sometimes people make the same mistakes repeatedly and expect a different outcome. I think that if we do not learn from our mistakes, and are willing to improve on them then that can lead to the feeling of failure. Failure is not something we want to feel, it is accepting that we have been defeated. We should all want to succeed and not be defeated by any situation.

In identifying yourself it is more than just your name. Your name was chosen for you, but you are the one choosing the characteristics that identifies you. We are not identified by one layer of our life, but all layers complete us. We are driven by our inner purpose. It is always important to know who you are. We are not just a name or any other title that people assign to you. We are who we have set out to become. We need to be confident with each choice we make, that it is made for our own legacy in identifying ourselves. We *need to expand our inner self and improve in the areas that we may be weak in. It is important to know always that our society is not in control of our own life. We should take control and live each experience proudly. It is how we live our life in every aspect that others will remember us by. The way we impact others will be how they will remember you. What type of legacy do you wish to leave behind? It is really up to you, for you are the one who has complete control of how you make every decision, and influence the lives around you. It is time to show society who you truly are.*

Chapter 2: *Society's level of income and how it affects who you are.*

*H*ave you ever met someone for the first time, and next question out their mouth is what you do for a living. This question asked repeatedly is what inspired me to write this book. What I do for a living is not who I am. I am a surgical technician by profession, but that is not who I am. I enjoy what I do; I enjoy helping take care of patients and helping others. My job is not glamorous I know. I am low man on professional ladder by society. I am treated as such by surgeons, nurses, and everyday society. Sometimes I know when I gear up with scrubs, hat, shoe covers, and a mask all is showing is my eyes. Sometimes I even wear tented safety goggles so you do not even see my eyes. I think it is because even though I am experiencing my task on hand I am not recognizable at all. I like that sometimes because that is not who I am. My job is a part of my life and I do enjoy it. I am a person inside all that gear, and only people who care to know me, will get a chance to know me.

I have worked with surgeons for years and they did not even know what I look like, much less who I am. I worked closely with one surgeon for many years who did not even know my last name, much less who I am. I worked close and scrubbed cases every week that surgeon came. I gave him a hard time about it, and he now knows my last name.

Recently I had helped a surgeon through a tough case, and not just me but a whole surgical team. He left the room then came back in. He asked the resident who had helped if he wanted box tickets for a baseball game that evening. The resident already had plans, and surgeon replied; "I was looking for someone to take the tickets, they are great seats, and do not want them to go to waste." Instead of asking rest of surgical team, I suppose he threw them away. See in society there are different levels of income. If you do not fit in their level of income, you do not exist. I am not sure I would want to exist in some people's life, when you are nothing any ways. I just was appalled, that someone would rather throw away box tickets to a baseball game, then to offer them to anyone else. It is hard to imagine for anyone to say in a room full of people, who just had helped you, "I wish I knew someone" as if we were no one

I think it is interesting how people with different income treat people differently. It works both ways like someone with lower income do not usually interact with someone with a higher income. It also works in a reverse pattern people with higher income do not socialize with people of a lower income. Wealth should not be measured by the amount of money we own. I think why we do not interact with people with different levels of income, is that we are afraid of what people might think or say. Often time people are treated for the one aspect of their life.

I have always tried to set goals to achieve certain things in life. Goals are future experiences of your wishes or desires. I remember one time my wife and I had set aside a goal to celebrate our tenth wedding anniversary with a nice trip. We went to the U.S. Virgin Islands and spent a week on St. Thomas. This was an awesome trip. I enjoy vacations for you get to spend time with who you want, and do what you want, when you want. You are usually living a simpler life without everyday distractions. It gives you a chance to realize that every day task is just tasks. There is more to life than just mindless activities that hinder us from being honest to our complete identity of who we are. I recall telling one of my friends about the trip. This friend materialistically makes a better income than me. I remember the way he treated me was as if I did not deserve to have a nice vacation because of my income. He insinuated that my trip was nicer than the one he had just been on. He indicated that because his *career provided him with a better income that he deserved to have better life than myself. I do not live every day of my life like we did that week. We had saved our money so we could enjoy ourselves, for this is a goal we achieved. A better life is not bought with money; it is bought with becoming sincere in knowing and living your life to your fullest potential. People should not focus on someone's income and place their standards or values on their career alone. A person should be validated for their actions of who they are and not just the amount of money they make.*

I have mentioned how I am treated differently because of my career. I experience this in a different perspective as well. People are sometimes treated differently because of the role they have, and not for who they truly are. An example is when surgeons that I work with are treated differently because of their career. Often times it is not genuine. People are only reacting to their role, and not to them as an individual person. Everyone is so intrigued by authority or roles in society, more than knowing or learning individuals for who they are. I suppose being in my role on the professional ladder and being low man may have its benefits. For if someone expresses interest in interacting with me it is usually sincere, and is not an act just because of my profession. I would rather have a sincere relationship and not an interaction for just my career. I often see the same behavior with bosses or managerial positions as well. So often the people in these roles do not even realize that other people are just reacting to the one aspect of their life, and not to them as a whole. They often think everyone thinks they are so great when in reality people are just reacting to the role they see, and not the person that they are. I often imagine do they even know what it is like by just being treated in a normal fashion. Sometimes I hear them complain of how they have been treated poorly, and I think that is way most people are treated on a daily basis. Often times it is the way that they treat others as well, and are just unaware of their behavior. When people are treated in same manner repeatedly they think that must be who I am. Is it really you, or is it what society has created for you to become? They are so use to being on center stage or center of attention, that they lose sight of how they should conduct themselves in a sincere manner. They are so dependent of who in society reacts to them, that when one does not interact then they cast them out or view them very poorly. They fail to realize not everyone is as impressed as what they are of their materialistic goals. Money sometimes can be a determining factor for their interactions. Their goals should be set for their true inner self, and not what others have chosen for them.

  Everyone wants to be successful, however, what is it that they want their success to be focus on? I think success in knowing who you are and keeping focus on your purpose in life should be a top priority. People often lose their priorities to society's image of success, and not their own personal goals. Often times people have trouble relating with people who may not be on the same economical balances as themselves. They presume that association of such caliber would affect their social image. They love being on center stage and will not allow the act to be taken away from themselves. They fail to realize that we commoners can see that their whole existence is just an act and it is not the reality of who they are. I witness this show time and time again. This is just another rerun that our society has created for our entertainment. I am getting bored by their poor acting, how I wished it was more of a reality show. Reality is allowing the truth to reveal itself in current times. I feel real time is better, than what society's image of people on center stage acting, or pretending to be someone that they are not, or could never be. Have you ever seen a movie repeatedly to the point that you know every line and every scene, after a while you just loose interest. I often feel our society's image of success is like these movies we just get to see different people playing the parts. Life is not a show I know. I wish some people could realize that center stage of society's image of success is not where we all identify our success. Success should be inner driven to our own personal purpose in life. Often time people start at the same personal level. Through repeated experiences from society of their role they are either built up or torn down, until you no longer match or connect at the same personal level. The way we react to these situations allow us to be someone we may be able to identify with or not.

I suppose the people that are built up feel as if they are at the top of the world. Top of the world is where the pollution accumulates and it is so hard to see things clearly. In life it is important to identify and realize the importance of your surroundings and how that you impact others. For being able to see yourself clearly allows you to direct your own life in the direction that can impact others in a successful way. Being true to whom you are intended to be is a successful start to your inner happiness and in identifying who you are in its entirety.

I once was diagnosed with sleep apnea. Before I was diagnosed I would drive to and from work sometimes not even remembering how I got there. I would fall asleep at traffic lights. My wakeup call is when I was woken to a horn blowing, because I was driving in someone else's lane. I have been treated for my apnea. I have noticed a huge difference. I cannot imagine my life before having surgery. I feel so much more alert now.

Just like driving my truck with apnea, sometimes in life we do not realize how we have gotten to certain areas of our life. There are not always horns to wake us up to realize we need help. I think a lot of times we are in a situation, that we sometimes do not understand the reason why. Sometimes we find ourselves asking how we ever got in this situation to begin with. In these times it is important to realize we may not always understand every aspect of each situation. Sometimes it is a preparation for what is yet to come. Often it is how we react that builds a positive foundation for situations that may arise in the future.

Sometimes people even have trouble identifying themselves. It is a huge step to realize that the inner person you had once known has changed. We should try to reunite with that inner person that makes us happy once again. Always remember anything is possible. Sometimes we have to take steps that may be difficult at first to achieve the inner goals we have for ourselves.

I am amazed at how other people are not even clear on their own perception on life. Often I feel that people choose to live a lifestyle on pure suggestion or something that may have been spoken to them in their life. The power of words is able to build some people's pride to an unrealistic standard. It also can tear down other people's pride in knowing who they truly are. Words can be a powerful tool it is how we choose to express ourselves that develop us each into an image of truthfulness of our inner thoughts. I think often we should evaluate our words before they are spoken and think of how it may impact the lives around you. Some people you could tell or suggest they are a queen or a king and sadly enough in their minds they are a queen or king. They become a queen or king and feel that others should bow and praise their unrealistic lifestyle. They believe they are in charge of their castle and that rest of society is their servants. They feel that they should be praised for their new unrealistic discovery. They feel as if they rule even who you are in reality they are just living a simple fairy tale themselves. They have no concern of how their actions affect others. They often feel as if they are the only one who can accomplish certain tasks, even if it takes a team of great people to accomplish these tasks. They will take all the credit for they are royalty. Suggestion in conversation does not make you a person you are not. I find these people to be weak in knowing and living who they truly are. Often people want to be known by their pretend or fairy tale identity instead of their own identity. It is obvious they have identified their weakness or else they would have no desire for change. People would be better off using their energy to better themselves for identifying their true inner self instead of persuading others of their dream character. I would be cautious of anyone who lives a life of lies and pretends to be a superior over others. I suppose we will always have people who believe they are truly royalty. They feel that pretending is more glamorous or accepted by others than the life that they should be living. I suppose peoples focus on income and success that alters their own identity to become a acceptable image to others. People may perceive you as a queen or king. This may not be as the royalty that you are seeking for there are all kinds of ways to end this title. I tell you the only person that should rule your kingdom is yourself. It is a pathetic lifestyle to live a life of words of suggestions and not a lifestyle that is true to your own purpose. One may wear a crown and even be in a pretend world, but at end of the day you are just who you are. Be in control of your own kingdom and do not let others rule who you are.

Recently I was at work and one surgeon asked me if I was going to lunch, and I replied yes. I sat with him at his table, and rest of the day all my coworkers were giving me such a hard time because I sat at his table instead of with them. I was not going to be rude and besides I did not see what the big deal was. I have a great work relationship with him. I am trying to get to know him for who he is, and not what he does. I have worked with him for twelve years and he is not liked by a lot of people for he is not always sincere, but I try to find the good qualities in him. We all have a good quality, sometimes we have to look harder to find it. I recently have tried to include him in my circle of friends. I do not have a lot of friends. This is one of my goals. Friends mean you have taken time to learn people for who they are. I have always built walls and let only few people in that friend circle. This is what I call an M&M friendship. M&M friendship is where one has a hard shell for protection. I was afraid of getting hurt I am learning to expand my circle which I have to learn people for who they really are.

I recall once a nurse told me that I was a "J.A.T." I ask what a "J.A.T.?" is "Just a tech" she replied. I am use to being treated that way; however, no one has ever called me that. I am now able to say I am more than a "J.A.T." I am a person who knows that there is more to life than what I do for a living. This is the same nurse that made a comment about me. A friend had made a cape that had said "S.T." my friend said it stood for "Super Tech. "When this nurse saw it she ask what does it stand for "Stupid Tech?" I recall my last day on that job this same nurse was yelling at me. I did not relieve her when she thought that I should. She was screaming it was my fault that her kids did not like her. I think I know why they did not like her. I did not care much for her either, especially when she started throwing chairs at me. All I can say is it seems some people are not worth my time and energy. We all know people like this I am sure. Even if it seems that someone is not worth your time everyone has a good qualities even this nurse. It is important to look always for the good in people around you, even if it is difficult to find. We should build on the good; we may be the only positive force in their life. Maybe by seeing a positive force in you they may decide to make their own inner goals to become a better person. The nurses at my current job treat me with respect, and put me on same level as them. We use the team approach no big "I" and little "u." They are worth my time and energy.

   Everyday society does not know much about my job. Soon as I tell them it always the same expression, it is "OH" then the conversation is over. That is why I do not like telling people what I do. Usually I get to tell my name shake their hand, before the conversation ends, at my choice of my career. I know people think I must be strange since I work in operating room. They do not care to learn more about who I am. I am still trying to figure out why I have to be treated different, because what I do and not who I am. A person is not the career that they do, but it is the inner person that so many people do not even give a chance.

I recently reached out to a person as a friend he was going through tough times. He was in process in moving to a different state. I tried to include him in my plans and make him apart of both my family and friends events. He was extremely appreciative. I am so glad I could be there as a friend. Even if I knew that getting closer would make it that much harder when he left town. I am just glad I could help someone through their tough times, and be a true friend. I suppose finding the inner part of me, and wanting to help out at any cost is a part of who I am. I am glad that I am still figuring out things about myself all the time. In the past I might look at "why be there for him he is leaving town and what difference could I make any ways." Now I feel I am a stronger person for being there. Exercise your inner self it will help you identify who you are.

I met a young man the other day. We started talking. He told me a lot about his life in just a few minutes. He told me that he was a single dad and had a four year old daughter. His wife was killed in a car accident when his daughter was one year old. The daughter was in the car and two other kids, the kids luckily were fine. She was on her way to pick him up from work. I ask him where his daughter was now. She was with his sister and he said by now probably with his in laws. He said they were like parents to him. I told him that it was great that he still included his in laws in the care of his daughter, because it will be good for her, and I am sure they see their daughter in his daughter's life. He also told me that his own dad was not involved in his daughter's life. I told him in regarding his dad, that it was his dad's loss. He also told me about how he was going to propose to a young girl over a weekend many years ago. Her brother called in the middle of that week, and she as well was killed in a car accident. I found out more in just the few minutes from this young man, than some of the people I have worked with for years. I found out a lot about him without even asking him what he did for a living. Just by listing and reaching out one can gain so much from each other.

      Maybe after we meet someone we should ask them to tell us about themselves. See how much you can learn about that person and who they really are, and not focus or judge them for what they do. I know a lot of times we are driven by money, however, that is not who a person is just because they make a lot of money. It does not make them a great friend. Most of my close friends are not wealthy, and they seem more content with themselves. It seems the more money a person makes, the more they spend, and the more miserable that person is.

      I work around a surgeon who is very successful in a professional sense, however, he always appears as if he just lost his best friend and appears miserable. This is the same surgeon who has been known to say "He fixes God's mistakes." So are you wondering why he is miserable now? If someone can talk about how God makes mistakes, then I am not sure that they will even bother to get to know anyone. Really to know a person you must be willing to be there for them, and not point out all the mistakes. We all make mistakes it is important to acknowledge them, and grow from them. Just because someone is successful in their professional career, does not automatically make them successful in whom they really are.

You may encounter great people professionally. A successful person is not always measured on how much money or the materialistic things that person has. I would rather have someone who will be there for me no matter what. The other thing I have noticed is the more money a person makes the less time that they have for themselves, and forget about spending time with you.

In texting people, the successful professional person will most of the time not even respond, not unless it benefits them. The circle of friends can be tested through texting. If a person does not bother to text you back, and you see them texting other people back on a regular basis. This sends me a message without even texting a word. That is they do not even want to be bothered by you. Often people treat text messages the way they would junk mail or a piece of trash by deleting it instead of responding with dignity. I think everyone deserves respect of a response of some capacity. Reality is reality and again on the professional ladder I am on the low side. Money is not a big attractor for someone who is at the top, and cannot be bothered by little me. That is fine; I would rather have friends who are willing to be there for me, than friends who only care about materialistic things anyways.

Today people have so many ways of media socializing. They often fail to have face to face conversations anymore. They are so focus on electronic socializing that real time seems to be falling by the wayside. This is such a great disappointment, for people are losing sight of true compassion and respect. I suppose it is their way of controlling the conversations in manner of whom they really want to interact with. They only respond to the most important ones. One may choose the path they want, and become a person who truly cares about their friends. Or one may choose to respond through an impersonal electronic device. We have so many ways through modern technology to improve our life, but do we? With media communication such as "Twitter or Facebook even texting and e-mailing" these are just a few examples. It is time we put "person" back into personal in all our efforts. Often after using these ways of communication people have already commented to you by same avenue. Once they see you in person they don't have anything to talk about anymore; in a more personal way. Are people just commenting on these types of avenues to avoid a more personal way of communication? You can choose to hide behind current technology, and never seem to become personal. Some people do not even use these avenues of communication and yet they still carry out the same behavior. I would like to encourage everyone to have a more personal interaction with others. It is time we each reach out with our own personal touch and become confident in who we are. There is a time to share and there is a time to ask others to share their experiences with you. I know in our life it is very personal to ourselves and is an exciting experience. We must realize there are also others who are excited about themselves. We never get to know about them, because we do not reach out to discover them on a personal level anymore. Life is not all about you. We must be willing to discover others and allow their identity to magnify in our life as well.

      People need to realize the way we treat others is an investment. The quality of our interactions with others will reflect on you individually. People perceive you as an individual from the interactions they receive over a period of time. We should strive for a strong investment, and not a temporary reaction to just get by. By treating others with respect and dignity is a start to a solid investment. If someone was buying of a materialistic item, they would expect the best quality for their money. To receive best from others you must be willing to give your best. By treating others in the way you would like to be treated is important process in achieving a great interaction in return. People often respond to others in the same manner that they are treated. I often believe that what goes around comes around.

By setting realistic expectations of others will keep you focused on what is achievable. By setting unrealistic expectations only frustrate both yourself as well as the other person. Sometimes we have to take a look at each situation, and evaluate it in a positive manner. There are many levels of expectations. We have to encourage some, while others will be the ones encouraging you. We each are an investment of who we are, and what we can contribute to society in a successful manner.

Chapter 3: *Doing the right things no matter what others may think about us.*

Part *of becoming aware of who we are, is willing to do the right*

thing no matter what people around you may think. We live in a judgmental world. People are so eager to find something wrong or different about you, and how people love to share that information with others. Things are not always what they seem. We are faced with decisions on a moment to moment basis. What we choose to do with these choices can affect others for the good or for the bad. I know there have been many times I have said or done things I wish I could have taken back. I have also said or done things that were taken out of content, and was not my intent. Nevertheless whether I have made a bad decision or something was taken out content. Someone has observed it, and they have taken note you can be assured of that. Once you start developing a pattern of either good or bad it is easier to follow these patterns, so it is pertinent to make good choices. If all people see is bad then you will be perceived in a bad category, not where anyone wants to be. It is important to acknowledge your mistakes, so you can grow from them, and become a better person. I think we all have that desire to do good things; it makes us feel good when we do them.

      Have you ever been out to eat or in a public place and see two people of same sex sitting together you automatically think they must be gay. If that is your preference I am not judging you it just a statement. The other way to look at it is if you see a man and woman sitting at a table you automatically think they must be an item as well. Not always the case maybe someone is going through tough times, and just needed someone to talk to, or maybe it's the others persons birthday or could be a multiple reasons why. We always think intimate relationships. There are all types of relationships. Why are we always reading more into things than what they are?

      My wife told me the other day after I was complaining about how I do not have any guy friends. She told me "it is because I never try to make plans with them; I might need to be the one who initiates it." When I try to initiate it I am rejected in some form of an excuse. I work with primarily women all day and come home to a house full of women. It would be great to hang every so often with guy friends. The guys I do work with are from a different economic balance from myself. They are not in the same mind set as me. It is as if I am not accepted in their world. This at times can be very frustrating and humbling. I am constantly trying to improve my social skills and present myself friendly to others. It is very challenging to move forward with a friendship when you receive information that reflects that the other person does not want to be bothered. I definitely do not want to be a pest or a bother to others. I find myself often going in a bungee type interaction. This is where I try to interact and yet I am jerked back into reality of no mutual desire of developing or advancing to a more sincere friendship. It is very difficult to adopt a friendship with others if there is not a mutual desire. Often times I am the only one initiates any type of communication. The response I do get back is usually out of pure obligation to respond back and often not sincere. I often feel having friends is a pretend world for me it is like I have imaginary friends. The only difference is that they do exist; the only thing imaginary about them is their friendship. They claim or even I claim them to be a friend, however in reality they are just nice people responding to your nice behavior. Friendship is developed over experiences that mold you into a better person that is enjoyed by the presence of each person. Great friends are intuitive to your needs and meet or surpass them. They will be there for you in the most trying times to support or encourage you. My value for friendship is someone who is sincere and true to themselves as well as to me. I think it would be fair to say that a friendship is not for one person; it should be that both parties, each would want to initiate some type of communication individually. I suppose I will learn to adapt my life into my purpose in this situation. I feel at times that it must not be meant for me to enjoy this type of friendship. This experience has made me realize how important it is for me to be happy within myself in knowing who I am.

      I see my wife go to have dinner at least once a week with friends from work. I would love to have that same type of "wind down" on occasion. I do not like sports, which I know limits my conversation with most guys because that is all they speak, breath, and live. I know my lack or desire of sitting and wasting hours upon hours watching someone else play games excludes me from a lot of conversations. I rather spend my time doing anything else. I sometimes do not get the purpose of the hours spent watching others play. I think a lot of people watch because it was a dream of their own. Some people watch just to be able to talk about it at the water cooler. I prefer to spend my time making my own dreams come true. Sometimes at work it can be annoying because in our break room all is on is the sports channels. I think it is funny because they repeat the same clips over and over again; and each time my coworkers get excited, as if they have already forgot about it, since last timed they viewed it. I think, I am only in here a few minutes for break and at lunch I am seeing the same thing and they are saying did you see that. I am thinking yes several times already and yet it never gets old for you does it. This behavior reminds me of a Labrador retriever you throw a ball and they retrieve it, they will do this all day and get excited each time as if it is their first time. I never have seen something so repetitive and the results have not change be so entertaining. Most of time they had just watched the game the day before, yet they must see it one more time. It is like television for someone who has trouble retaining information. I prefer to be doing something anything instead of throwing my valuable time away sitting and watching sports. What is even worse wasting valuable time watching clips or highlights of games that one has already wasted time on. I honestly do not see how a person devoting hours upon hours of time watching these games get anything done for themselves. I would rather be playing sports than watch these overpaid athletes. I suppose I am more of a doer than a watcher. I think in identifying yourself one must learn to be able to do things for oneself.

  I would like share a story about a teenage boy. He was in high school and had long hair. Just by looking at him you would think he was not a good kid or a problem child. The truth of matter was that he intentionally grew his hair long, so he could donate it. That is a great gift. My daughter grew her hair to donate as well. I am sure as a guy he went through a lot of grief. Great example of how one is willing to do the right thing no matter what others may think. That teenage boy has a great start in finding who he really is, better yet I think he has found who he really is, and is a living example for everyone.

I recently attended a wedding, my wife's friend from work. I am glad I got to know them. They are great people. The husband had a previous relationship, and his girlfriend at that time had a four year old son, and the father of that child was not in the picture. This child is an interracial child which to me is not that uncommon, by society this can be judged differently. He took that child as if he was his own. This child is not any blood relation, and he takes him still every other weekend. He is impacting that boy's life in a very positive way. I am sure he has encountered some judgmental opinions from people, who do not even know the situation. He also had a child with that previous relationship, and his wife has two sons as well. He is a Dad to all four of them. He is a great person and would do anything for any one of these boys. Great example of how it does not matter what others may think, that good people will do the right thing.

Doing good things should not lead into bad thoughts, however, by our society it sometimes does. I like to share with you one of my experiences with you. Recently at my work someone had done something nice for me. I went home, and told my family about it, and my ten year old when she found out it was a male, she replied "he must be gay." I was disturbed for she has never met him, and did not even know any aspect of his life, other than his act of kindness. I told her he was not gay. This is not something I have taught my kids, however, the influence that society has on our kids can impact the way that they react. I think it is very interesting how my wife is able to buy flowers or do an act of kindness for another woman. How someone does an act of kindness for her and these types of thoughts never enter people's mind. If a guy does something kind for another guy our society automatically thinks thoughts just like my youngest daughter. I do not think we should alter our good works because of our gender, age, religion, race, or any other things that our society forms judgment on. I think sometimes males are expected to carry a rough and tough image. People feel that kindness is a sign of weakness, and is not an image that guys should be associated with. I think often times this hinders a lot of people from doing the kind things that other people deserve. Everyone has a reputation that has taken their entire lives to build. People worry about one person destroying that image. When people do kind things people automatically jump to conclusions that it must be an intimate relationship. We all should be able to do good deeds and not worry about what others think. We should be able to do good deeds because we want to do good. It is our intentions followed by our actions that should direct us in the right direction. Just because we do something good does not make us a weak person. Lot of people look at being kind as being weak, however, I disagree I think it is a strength. I feel that being a positive force for you as well as for others is the way we *should all set our goals in any relationship and not worry about what society judgment thinks. It is so easy to fall into our society's mentality. We should not allow society to set standards for ourselves to achieve. We should set our own standards or goals to achieve. We should focus on doing the right things no matter what. Our first priority should be to ourselves. We should be a positive force and an example for ourselves as well as others. We can make that difference in our lives if we conduct our every behavior in a positive manner. We have complete control of our direction that we take in life. We can live our life in a direction that we can be proud of and others will want to achieve for themselves. The direction we choose is determined every day by the decisions that we make. That is why we should always be mindful of our actions and always strive to improve ourselves to become the best positive force possible in every aspect of our life.*

Change is something we experience every day. Change is just a part of life. With every change there is a decision that must be made, and how we react to each one of these choices can impact you in who you are. We will always have a choice in each situation. We can always choose what is right. The path that we choose may make an impact on you, as well as others. Your previous experiences have developed your mindset of who you have already become and help you build the choices that you are currently facing. We are constantly building our own personal perspective on life; each choice we make builds on the next. These changes affect who we are, and who we should become. In every choice we make it is imperative to try to make them a positive one that matches with your personal inner goals. Striving to do the right thing no matter what the rest of society thinks. It is what is within that truly matters. The more we try to do good things the easier it is and the better we will feel about who we are. Being there for family and friends in a time of need, no matter what others may perceive, is essential for who you are. We exercise to keep in great shape just as we exercise to keep physically fit. We also need to exercise our inner self by doing a self-evaluation. When we make mistakes we need to learn from them and allow them to improve who we are. By constantly doing mental exercise and improving yourself will help you become a better person, and a stronger person as well. Each decision we make can impact our lives as well as others. Be proud of who you are, and to feel good about yourself. If you do not like yourself how do you expect others to like you as well? If you are unhappy with yourself then it is time to make a change and become the person you can be happy with. Happiness is an essential part in everyone's life. It is more fun to be happy than to not be enjoying yourself.

Sometimes it may seem difficult to do the right thing. I am not able to grasp the concept of violence we hear about on a daily basis. Seems our society has taken a change over time. We have experienced so many tragic stories. I have heard of some stories where someone has heard of a plot of violence and they turn the person or persons *into authorities. This is example of someone doing the right thing. This may be difficult for I can imagine that it would be scary to do, for the fear of the violence may be focused on you. Tragic stories have been altered by these heroic acts. My mind is not able to comprehend the violence and the satisfaction a person thinks they can receive by doing such awful acts. I think we need to be aware of our surroundings always and keep our guard up. It seems places that were once seemed safe now is being targeted by violent actions against innocent people. If you ever think that you may have these violent tendencies, I would like to challenge you to identify the reason for these feelings. If a person knows the reason why these feelings exist, it will be easier to address them. Try to eliminate these awful feelings before these feelings take over your whole being. If someone has done bad thing to you, it does not give you a reason to tragically execute your awful behavior. If a person you know needs help then please help them. Talk to someone if you need help in helping them. There are no problems to big that cannot be resolved. Violent actions do not need to be taken. Violence and tragedy are not the answer to any problem. These awful actions will never make anyone a hero. A hero is someone that helps people, not someone who executes violent actions. We encounter heroes on a daily basis. So many times these heroes blend in until the opportunity arises to prove themselves. It is great to know that a hero do not arise only in a violent situation. Heroes are willing to help anyone at any time without receiving* recognition for their heroic actions. There have been so many heroes in my life. I suppose we all have a choice in our life to be someone's hero. Being a hero is a special privilege that should not be taken lightly. A hero does not wear capes and fly around; they are people who are true to their purpose. They are willing to take their purpose a step further to help human kind. It is much better to be perceived as a hero than a villain. We sometimes lose sight of our surrounding in our society. We let our guard down and let the villains blend in our society as well.

      Villains are people seeking to execute violent actions or tragic outcomes. Villains are simply living their own lives as a disturbed or unstable individual. It seems villains often think they are the hero when they act out their vicious crimes. It seems that they seek recognition for their actions. Villains' lives often end in the same tragic manner as they plan to execute on others. What is the purpose for all of these evil activities, when nothing seems to be carried out as a beneficial outcome for anyone involved including the villain. I think there are so many ways of expressing your point than taking innocent lives or harming others. These are foolish actions for often times the reason for these actions are not even understood. These actions are not being set for any reason, when the reason these villains set their goals are not even accomplished. Often people are left trying to make sense of these vicious actions. In reality these actions make no intelligent sense at all. The villains have failed their reasonable sense *once again. Their life is now remembered as a failure by everyone. Is this how anyone wants to be remembered? It is a shame they cannot work their issues out before they lose control of their whole being. They should face their problems instead of angrily act out such violently tasks. I think it is important to realize their problems before they lose all efforts of sanity.*

It is time to put human back into humanity and realize the importance of each life, and not just their life. Violence is a serious problem that we all need to identify and attempt to change. We all can do our part, and it can start with awareness. We as a society need to realize we have a serious issue that needs addressing. This is not just a problem for the victim's families left to contend with. We all need to be more heroic to the idea of resolving this huge problem. We are enduring violence in places that in the past we felt were safe. If you ever encounter an issue or a suspicious behavior report it to someone who can help in the matter on hand. I think together we can make a difference. We are worth every effort that it takes to help someone who is disturbed enough to creates violence. It is time to be a hero to the villains, so they can see that there is a different way of dealing with problems than through their violent tendencies.

My heart, prayers, and thoughts go out to each family who their loved one has been taken away by these awful crimes. I do not have the talent of words to express in these difficult times. I think we all should remember these precious lives. Together we can build awareness of violent issues and hopefully stop the violence before it stops another life. We each have a choice to live, a life to be proud of and help others become aware of their heroic attributes. We all should strive to do the right things no matter what others may think.

Chapter 4: *Relationships and how they affect who you are.*

There are all types of relationships. There is religious, parent to child, friendships, boyfriend to girlfriend, husband to wife, parent to child, coworker to coworker relationships. These are just a few examples of many types of relationships. Each relationship we encounter may happen differently with each situation. Who we surround ourselves can impact who you are. Not to say we cannot be who we are intended to be. If you surround yourself with positive people then it easier to be a positive person yourself. In certain situations you are the positive person and it is very important to leave *that positive influence as your legacy. In life you never know when you are just living your life as everyday experiences can change the way a person feels about themselves. You could be the changing point for someone to identify who they are.*

Religious relationships can be very challenging for me. Even if I attend the same religious place every time it is available to attend, I may interpret things in a whole different light than someone sitting right next to me. I do believe in God and all his great works, and believe each of us is a part of his plan. I feel that a religious belief is a personal decision that we as individuals have to make. Have you ever been around people who think they are holier than God himself? I do not like being around these type of people. I often think that some people are more focus on religion than their beliefs. I think the basics of our beliefs should be what is important. The way people choose to direct their lives is not always in proper alignment of their basic beliefs. We should conduct ourselves in a better manner through our beliefs, but do we? I think it is important to have a close relationship with God, and to try living a life that other people can see a difference in you. In my life, I have witnessed religious people are quicker to judge you than anyone else, and are willing to gossip about their new discovered sinful person. In everyday society people seem more accepted of who you are. It may seem strange that God's people would be more knowledgeable about the fact that we are all human and that everyone makes mistakes, yet they are the first to cast judgment.

Forgiveness is a huge step and sometimes it may be difficult. We should be able to forgive someone whether it has been ask or not ask from the person that offended you. During the forgiveness stage, at any point, if you feel you need to talk to that person that should be encouraged. In any type of relationship communication is so important. Sometimes we may need to bring up things that are difficult to bring up and it may be painful to us. It is important to communicate to them so that they know the areas where they need to improve and set inner self goals, so they can become a better person.

I want to share with you my own experience with a conflict that involves a religious relationship. This person who offended me was someone that I grew up with. This person is very good at talking to others and sometimes can be persuasive. This individual did some bad works against my family. I felt his intent was not of God or his plan. I had pulled away from my upbringing of almost thirty years to relocate my family into a better situation. I had separated my life from this individual for over ten years. This was extremely hard on me and I could not understand why my family had to be the ones to relocate from my childhood place of worship, when I felt I had been the one victimized. I got angry at God, not a place I would recommend but it was the truth. I could not see the purpose of all the evil activities that had taken over in my life. I even made a promise to God on my terms and not of God's purpose. My promise was that I would never plan to involve myself with this individual until he apologized to my family.

To my knowledge this individual to this day has not apologized. I got angry at God once more when this individual started attending my current place of worship. I was so angry I could not understand. I think I hated this individual, again not God's will. I even contemplated the purpose to even attend a place of worship at all, if that was what was going to happen was evil follow me. I thought this individual cannot come to my house and maybe that is where I should be. Once this individual started attending regularly I started asking God to allow me to be more accepting of this individual. I eventually learned to forgive this individual without him asking for forgiveness and we now talk regularly.

In my life forgiveness took over where I thought it was impossible. It took this individual to work at it as well. I know we may never be best friends, even if we did grow up together, our paths are not the same; however, we accept each other for who we are. Through this experience I feel stronger and better about myself for through forgiveness anything is possible.

No matter what life situations we encounter we should make the best of them and try to learn and grow from each one. By living a religious life you will know who you are, and what you are to do with yourself, and let God be your guide for he has a bigger plan for you, than what you could even imagine. It is important to know your inner self and keep it, as pure as possible. Living a pure life can be challenging at times, but the rewards God gives us each day make it worth all the effort. We have an awesome God who deserves our full attention. I know I could never repay my God for all the many blessings he blesses me with each day. The least I can do is keep a pure life and give him the praise that he so greatly deserves. Without God I know none of us would be who we are today.

Since I can remember my parents were there to guide me and teach me from right and wrong. All their parenting has helped me develop into the man I am today. They did a great job raising me as well as my older sister and brother. There is a certain amount of where there parenting kicks in, and a certain amount that is me and my personal decisions. I realize that there is my inner thought of who I am, and what I am to do with decisions that I am faced with from day to day. My dad had many sayings one of them he often told me, my brother, and my sister was "two wrongs do not make a right." I know in my life there are a lot of situations that occur or I am treated poorly but it does not mean it is right for me to retaliate.

Regardless if your parents were always there for you or not you must have had someone who stands out, someone that may have helped you to develop into the person you are today. I know in my different stages of my life there were different people around me to help me develop into who I am today.

Friendship is a wonderful thing to have. A friend is someone who is there for you through the good times as well as the bad. In life there are so many obstacles that we are faced with and it is great to know you can have someone to support you no matter what.

    I remember a time in high school when I surrounded my life with not such a great friend. He was a compulsive liar. I remember when we were a freshman and there was someone who was attacking people in the bathroom with a knife. I remember being scared to go to bathroom, afraid I would get attacked. My friend had already got attacked and another person that he was acquainted with. I thought; how am I to know I would not be next. I remember him asking a teacher if I could go to the bathroom with him to keep an eye out so he would not get attacked again. I, of course, did go to watch the doorway for him. I do not know what I was supposed to do if they came at me with a knife; however, I went to help a friend out. Later I found out that the whole story was made up and that the other boy and my friend had cut themselves with a knife. I was not very happy with the way I was involved with all that drama. I also recognized that this behavior is not who I wanted to become.

    The same high school friend had called me after he had gotten his license and ask if I wanted to go for a ride. I said sure. Once he got to my house the car was full of a lot of his friends. And so we all went on for a ride. It started snowing and he started speeding to get us all home. He did not get permission to drive the car from his parents. He did not even bring me all the way back home. I had to walk. He had to wipe down the car before his dad got home. As an adult I now look back of this experience and realize how fortunate we all were riding in that car full of teenage boys. So often we hear about teenagers that are in this similar situation and either they are seriously injured or even killed. We all probably have known people like this or have had experiences similar to this. Being true to you is as important to being truthful to others. Living your life in front of other people can be the positive force that they might need to realize they need to improve their own inner self. Being there for others is not just beneficial to them it also helps you in different circumstances and makes you stronger to achieve a positive outcome.

      Relationship that is intimate by you and another person. I think this is one of closest. A Spouse is a friend who has chosen to be with you for the rest of your life for better or worse. They have made a promise to you to always be there. I love my wife so very much. She tolerates a lot of my adventures or stress that I may bring to the household, and still loves me unconditionally. She is very thoughtful always giving to others before herself. She was like that before we had our two girls. She is definitely a positive force in my life. I do not know what my life would be like if I did not have such a strong partner to always be by my side. We are always together and we include each other in our plans. Communication is the key in any relationship and it is even more important in a marriage. There is not a day that we do not express our love for one another. She knows when I am down, and when there is something bothering me. She will make me talk about things even if I do not even want to talk. How can she support me if she does not even know what has been going on with me? Choosing a partner to spend the rest of your life is very important in identifying who you are. She is the love of my life and the rock of our family. She holds everything together. As a couple you are developing your world as unity which from this point on you will be identified together as one. It also identifies who you are.

As children come in the picture you will discuss a decision that now impacts a whole new life. Parenting together as one thought and process require communication and planning. My wife is the best mom to our girls. She is more than a parent she supports them, encourages them, and advises them in a lot of their activities. I know my girls will be strong women because of the support they have received their whole life. They have definitely been molded into who they are, and how they should carry out the many decisions that they will be faced with.

When my daughter was in first grade I used to pick her up from school on my days off. She would get into the truck and complain about how this one girl would mistreat her. This girl was not very nice to others, she developed a very negative impact at such a young age. I think this is very sad, for this girls influences in her life has directed her in a very negative path. Every time I would pick her up she would just complain. One day I told her after she complained that she had to tell me two good things that happen today to every one bad thing. I wanted to try to change her mind set so that she could develop into looking for good instead of all the bad things. I wanted for her to look for the positive in every situation. Looking for positive or good is something we all should live by. We are going to be faced with challenges in our lives, but we should be able to find good in them. This is one thing I wanted to instill in my daughter as a moral value at a young age.

When my oldest daughter was real young someone asked me a question. I recall the question being "did I feel that parenting a child influenced them as the person that they will become, or will they be who they are no matter what?" I feel parenting is very important. In early years we are to show our kids the difference from right and wrong, or good morals. I think as they get older they will experiment with their boundaries, and may even test them. I feel as parents it is our job to always reveal our expectations of them. It is important to be encouraging when they do follow these expectations, and express our disappointment when they are not met. It is important to have a discussion or advise them in the direction that is in proper alignment of our expectations. I do feel discipline a child is important it shows them their boundaries and when one passes these boundaries of expectations in a negative way there is consequences that one must face. This is a lesson that will carry them through life; for in everyday activities there are expectations that must be met. There are many ways to discipline a child it could be taking away something that they enjoy for a certain period of time. It could be giving time out for a period of time. Each child responds differently to different ways of discipline it is imperative to reveal your expectation as guidance of their wellbeing and to keep them safe. By communication to why they are being discipline shows them that we do have their best interest in our plans. By discipline a child it shows you do care about their actions. It is a way to implement good moral values in becoming successful of their identity. I do feel each person is an individual. We should set certain guidelines and allow them to make their own choices. We are to be there for them and to council them into the right direction. We have these guidelines for them to follow, and expect them to live their lives in a manner, that best matches our expectations. By having boundaries we are to allow a certain amount of freedom, and a certain amount of discipline that is balanced by their actions. We are to allow them to discover themselves as a supportive role as a young person in whom they truly are.

      Families that are close are molding their kids into whom they are by the different experiences that each family goes through. It is important to try to keep a positive relationship with your kids. I know different stages can be more challenging, however, they are very fragile as a child, and we want them to be strong as an adult and become knowledgeable of whom they are.

      Coworkers can sometimes be the most challenging relationships. The reason I feel it is so challenging is because you have so many different people involved, and each one has their own perspective on life. There is a range of maturity; at least with parenting my children I know they are young and are still adventurous on life's decision. In the work place I have decided that just because you are an adult does not always mean you act like one. I have witnessed a lot of diversity at work. We often spend more awake time with coworkers than we do with our own family and friends. We do not get to pick our coworkers. We have to present ourselves in a professional manner even if we do not like them. Sometimes in the work place we have more chiefs than Indians. Remember in the religious area, the holier than God himself statement I made, and how I do not like to involve myself around people like that? In the work place I cannot stand people who think they do no wrong, and everything they do is more superior to anyone else. I find that these people get isolated, because there is not anyone who wants to be around them, at least for the ones who can see it. That is defiantly not the person I would set my goals to be like. Coworkers, who believe that they are more superior to others, often vocalize their greatness. They fail to realize their greatness is better observed, than self-expressed. They do not have to promote themselves by praising their every detail that they do. In a work place actions speak louder than words. I would rather someone to show me what they can do rather than telling me what they can do. One should be known by their consistent experiences that they live. When one lives a great life others will know it, no one will have to tell them. I tend to distance myself from people who have to build themselves up to be someone that they are not. These people tend to tear down others to magnify their greatness. The only thing they magnify is their insecurity of whom they truly are. We are a team and should always remember that it takes all of us to complete tasks. There is a person that I work with that post devotional messages. I find no wrong with that. I find it interesting; however, the other day I asked help from this individual and they refused to help me as a coworker. One can read every devotional or inspirational message available; it is not until you apply these messages into actions that a positive change actually occurs. People often think just because they read something positive, makes them live a positive life. People may not remember something you say or do, they will remember the way you treat them, over anything else. There should not be little "u" and big "I" in the work environment. Unfortunately there is that mentality at times. I do take great pride in what I do and encourage others as well. My philosophy in teaching a new employee is to teach them all I know. I can teach all the knowledge I have; however I cannot teach experience. Experience is applying your knowledge and skills toward a certain goal incorporated into an interaction with others. In a work environment experience takes time. Often people want experience that has taken other people years to achieve. They want this experience before they leave orientation, this is just not possible. This expectation is not *realistic; it can be frustrating for this mentality to exist. By applying your skills you will develop your own experiences that will guide you in your career. Some people work for ten years and have ten one year anniversaries others work ten years and have ten years' worth of experience. It is all in the way one applies oneself. In life this lesson can apply to everyday experiences it is all in attitude and how one applies oneself.*

As a Surgical Technician I am use to being treated with little respect. I just do my best and try to keep a positive outlook. What people fail to realize is your career is not who you are. There is a person behind each job title created. Each person deserves to be treated by who they are, and not what title they have. In my line work I see this behavior all the time.

I work around surgeons who some are great, and some well I am trying to keep this a clean book. I know in my line of work there is a lot of stress involved. I respect the possibility that there is a lot stress on a person. Sometimes in life I lower my expectations of certain people, or situations. I am still disappointed in their interactions, even though I have a great respect for them as a person. I expect my interactions with certain people to not be most ideal. I think we should not let them lower our morals however. Sometimes no matter how well you treat others, the mutual respect will not be given back to you. It is so important in these situations to always keep your dignity, and not let these situations rule your purpose. Through multiple experiences we realize that not everyone is tuned into other people's lives, and are not concerned in trying to learn them either. By lowering my expectations of certain people it helps me to keep a positive outlook. I am not expecting to have a positive interaction, so when I do I am pleasantly surprised. If I do not have a great interaction then at least I had already prepared myself, and it is not so much of a great disappointment. Sometimes even when we do prepare ourselves for our interactions to go in a negative way, and it goes in a positive way. We should acknowledge it and thank the person for the positive experience. By thanking a person or acknowledging them it may make a person to realize that you do notice a difference, and hopefully they will want to make a positive change. In our own personal life we need to keep a positive outlook on life no matter how difficult a situation or a person may seem.

    I want to share some of my experiences with you. There is this one surgeon and I am close to him, and work hand in hand with for over twelve years now. I greatly respect him as a great surgeon. The way he treated me would have appalled most people. I am there to provide a service and to help during the cases as needed. I would try to communicate to him, and he would throw up his hand in my face, and say "I cannot talk to you right now, I am busy." This all took place before the cases even began. Then another physician would walk in the room right after telling me that, and he would start up a long conversation with them, this happen on numerous occasions.

Another time comes to mind as well with the same surgeon. Once I went away for vacation. When I came back he asked me how my vacation was. I started telling him about it, and again I got hand in face, and same reply "I am sorry I am busy." I just stood there thinking REALLY? You are the one who asked. That is example how other people choose to be friends with certain income levels or by titles. I am who I am and not what I do. Yes what I do is a part of what identifies me, but that is just a small part. I am so much more than a surgical technician. I love what I do, sometimes I wish I could be more involved in other people's life through conversation, and let people get to know me for who I am. I did discuss with this surgeon. How I did not like the way I had been treated. He apologized and told me he was unaware of doing that. In every relationship it is important to communicate. How is the other person to know what is on your mind?

No one likes to be taken for granted. So many times in my career I have seen people who are constantly being given things, and it never seems to be enough. I have found that the more that you do for other people the more that they want. They have been given so much that they lose track of who they really are. It is all about themselves, and what you can do for them. They just see you as their servants, and that is all that they want to know you as. I know in my career I often am look as the servant boy, I am more than a servant. I do provide a service and I do enjoy giving to others, however, there is more to me than just providing a service. Sometime in life it seems no matter how much you give it is never good enough. I find trying to become friends with someone like this can be extremely difficult. In any type of relationships there is you and someone else. If you are not good enough for them then it may seem impossible to become in any type of relationship with them. Exception to this would be if you are their service person, which over time can be degrading. If that is all you have in common is trying to help or please them, and never see anything in return. I hope in my life I will keep focus of people around me, and can be there for them always. Whether it is support they need, or someone to just listen. I think we all can improve on how we interact with each other.

  In society we are categorized in different areas of income or values, and do not give people the ample chance to be themselves. Every so often it would be great to have a genuine conversation, and not feel like you are being constantly taken for granted. Everyone deserves respect of who they truly are as a whole, and not just what that person is willing to do for you.

  I once was hired to start up a surgery center. It was a lot of hard work. I got to do things I never thought would be possible for me to complete. I was hired for the knowledge that I have. I was very diligent in every detail, and the surgery center is still very successful today. I had a major role in that, and I take great pride in the preparation of a prosperous surgery center. It was a great experience except the surgeons who had asked me to set up the surgery center that I greatly respect, never once was concerned enough about me to check and make sure everything was fine. I thought that through setting up, organizing, and ordering equipment and supplies that they might would check to see if everything was going okay, or if I needed anything. I experienced the service person mentality once again, that is so demoralizing. I do not like the feeling of being used. I think it would have felt better being appreciated and supported. I should be used to this feeling; however, I thought I was entering a new experience that could have been a positive one.

    I suppose I do provide service each day I just wished I could be valued or respected for who I am and not what I can do for you. It is not the giving part that I have a problem with. I enjoy giving; it is the mindset of the people that I help that bothers me. Especially the ones that are only are interested in the one aspect of what can I do for them. I am referring to people whom I work frequently with. Only have service interactions with them on a regular basis, and never a personal, or sincere response from them. I find that these types of people are so use to treating other people with the mentality of how you owe them. Getting to know you as an individual is absolutely out of the equation. If I was in the equation then I would at least be treated equal.

    Currently the medical director of this same surgery center was showing what appeared to be another doctor around. It appeared to be an interview. This medical director never once introduced this individual to the rest of the staff; it appeared as if we were just a service person to him. I know I am not there much; however, everyone else deserved the courtesy of an introduction. I also think if I was interviewing, and someone did not even introduce me to the people that I may have interactions with then this must be an impersonal place to work. Sometimes we send messages without speaking one word. Actions speak louder than words, and are able to send messages that are very clear. Service boy is not really use to being treated with genuine respect. I think being treated repeatedly in this type of environment has played a role in my everyday interactions. I am always trying to please others, and when someone finally treats me with respect I often find myself asking at what cost, or what reason? I find myself not feeling worthy of a lot of things that rest of society does not even think about, like just having a simple friendship. I have been used so many times just for one aspect of my life for the service that I can provide that over time it can impact your inner self if you let it. I believe this mentality has made it difficult for me to trust people, and their intent, in this type of situation. Trust is something earned through positive interactions with each other. I have to tell myself every time I am in these types of situations that I am more than what I am even given a chance. The people, who just want to know my service, are really the ones who are missing a great person in their life.

We all have greatness inside each of us, if we are just given a chance to share it. We are surrounded by great people, and so often times we do not even see it. We all have the potential of being a great person and it is what you do with it that makes a difference in the lives around you every day. Even though my career can be frustrating, and be very humbling, I still know that there is more to me than just the service that I provide. I hope that one day other people around me can see the whole me and not just what they choose for me. I choose my path. Not what they want me to be, but who I want to be.

Have you ever been to a dolphin show? After the dolphins perform they get rewarded with fish. Sometimes the dolphins get treated better than what we treat people around us. Getting rewarded ever so often with a genuine appreciation would be a positive gesture. Some people have not been genuine for so long, that they probably would need to do a long inner search to even be able to identify what it truly means to be a genuine person. People have learned to play a part, to receive what they want, not even caring how it may impact other people's life around them.

Remember we have many aspects in our lives that identify who we are. One aspect is not the only thing that identifies the inner person that we each have. In life we may have many trials and frustrations; it is how we handle each of them that make us stronger. Always know you have control over every situation. No matter what situation may arise just be yourself, and be happy in who you are.

Chapter 5: *What identifies you as who you are?*

There are many factors that identify who you are. What is important in your life would probably be the first item on your list. Your background raising or upbringing also identifies who you are. Your inner self is the biggest factor in who you are. What you do on a daily basis has some impact on who you are. How you handle difficult issues, and how you make a difference in your life as well as others surrounding you, also identifies who you are. The interest or hobbies you have help you realize what is important to you, and gives you a sense of peace in your life. What or who you are passionate about is an important factor in your life, and influences you in whom you are? People that have a major impact in your life; or that positive force in *your life have certainly made an impact on who you have become. There are so many different ways to identify who you are. The truth is only you know what is important in your life. The experiences you have been faced with, and who was there to see you through them. That is what identifies who you are. Always remember to be true to yourself and others. Truth will be revealed to others whether you realize it or not. People can see so much in your life. That is why it is important to live a life that you can be proud of.*

My dad has a saying that "it does not matter what you choose as a career, it does not matter if you are a ditch digger, but to be the best ditch digger there is." The moral of that saying is to take pride in what you do, and to do your very best at all that you do. I know your career is just a small part in identifying who you are; however, I think you can apply this same philosophy in any aspect in your personal life. Attempt to be the best at all you do, especially things that truly matter to you. When you take pride in everything you do, and it does not seem to go the way it should, it is comforting to know you have done your very best. In these times it is good idea to figure out what could have been handled differently, and try to improve for the next time. This is a way of constantly improving yourself by learning from your experiences. Sometimes the experiences we are faced with are the best teacher in life's many challenges. I am tougher on myself when things go wrong than what others around me may be.

I enjoy working in my yard and try to make the landscape to be pleasing to the eye. I find this a relaxing factor in my life and the reward is great you get the gratification of an appealing yard that others can see. Like my yard, my life is similar. The more I work at it and try to do the best I can the better it will become. I always hope it is a difference that not only I can see, but others that are in my life.

I recently had placed a koi pond in my back yard, a long dream of mine. I finally got my wife's blessings last summer. My wife told me if we were going to put a pond in it should go right here, as she was pointing to the area where I just finished my Japanese garden. This is the same garden that took over a year to complete. I did not hesitate I dug up every plant placed in containers kept them alive. That was not in my plan; however, sometimes you have to do whatever it takes to keep your dreams alive. We did the work ourselves with help from both sides of our family. After hard sweat it finally paid off. Once the construction was finished I already had all the plants needed to finish the landscape. I do not think I lost one of my transplanted trees and shrubs. It was amazing. The finished landscape around the pond is just stunning. Everyone who comes to my yard now is drawn to the pond and comments on how beautiful it is. It was a lot of hard work, however, in the end it was worth it. I find myself coming home every evening and relaxing, and enjoying my beautiful koi. My point is no matter what is placed in your life if it something you want to achieve, then it should be worth the effort, and the reward may be able to make an impact on not only you, but others as well. The things we can learn about ourselves through our hobbies are a big part of who we are.

      Another hobby of mine is photography. I think one reason I like it is there are only suggestions of how to take photographs. For me there are no set rules. Being able to capture a moment in time and record the image to share with others for years to come is a great gift. By looking at photos it can trigger our minds of a trip or of someone dear to us, someone you have not seen for a while, or inspire you to achieve a goal. I know I enjoy looking at the pictures in magazines, and getting ideas for my own hobbies. Sometimes it is images of people or a landscape that may inspire me to try it in my own yard. Some hobbies go hand in hand like mine. I enjoy outside activities like hiking, mountain biking, gardening, and photography. I often take a small camera on hikes because you never know what next bend may instill that inner thought. I have taken pictures on hikes, and try to mimic nature in my own landscape. Landscaping and photography is a way to record my improvements. I enjoy outdoor photography the best, it can be more challenging, because you are faced with light that is always changing it definitely not a studio where the environment is controlled. Challenges can be good. It gives you a chance to set goals, and a chance to achieve them, which makes us a little stronger. We can set goals every day, and at the end of the day we can grow from them, whether we met them or not.

Have you ever heard "what don't kill you makes you stronger?" I am proof of that saying. I was bullied by an entire bus to the point I could not imagine my life beyond that current situation. I know that this bus was not really killing me physically, but mentally it seemed to impacting me as if they were killing my inner self. I endured great deal of unnecessary suffering. I feel through this experience it has helped me to become aware of this serious problem. I hope to be able to help someone realize through my own perseverance, one is able to surpass any difficult situation; we will always be the stronger person in overcoming each obstacle. There are support organizations for bulling now like Rachel's Challenge that helps many kids in this serious problem. I encourage anyone to find support for either yourself or someone else if one is ever in this type of situation. We all need to do our part in this serious problem and be willing to address it. We each are here for a very important purpose. Each of us is a special person, who has a meaningful attribute to contribute to society.

I want to share my bulling story and identify my hero in this circumstance. I started middle school, and had to ride the high school bus. I was fine at first then in middle of the year they changed my bus route. The new bus was awful. I was greatly disturbed by the way I was treated on this bus. People were EVIL to me. I hated the ride on that awful bus, cried every day on the long walk home. I was the last one to be picked up in the mornings on this new route, and even though there were plenty of seats for me to sit in, I was not allowed by the kids on the bus. I recall some seats only had one person in them, and I still was not allowed to sit down for the ride to school. I would have to stand for the long ride to the middle school. I was made fun by all the kids on the bus. They would say things about me that was not true. They would spit on their fingers, and then place their fingers in my ear. I would just look out the window and try to escape mentally that miserable ride. I would just go numb after a while, for they were bad people. I did not ever want them to know they won. It is bad enough to be bullied by one person, but it seemed impossible for one person to withstand being bullied by a whole entire bus. I honestly do not know how I endured this awful behavior. I know this was a major molding for me, to always be considerate of other people's feelings, no matter what.

      One glorious day my bus driver told me to be at the bus route at an earlier time. From that day forward I no longer was the last person picked up but now the first. I still remember that first day of the change when the bus passed my road and the whole entire bus cheered, because they thought she had forgot to pick me up. I finally got a seat to ride to school. No one had to stand anymore for there were always plenty of seats. I will never forget what Mrs. Bise did for me that day. I am a grown man in my forties, and it is still painful when I recall the way I was treated.

Bulling is a serious problem, and should never be taken lightly. If you noticed I intentionally have not used names in my book until now. I feel Mrs. Bise is my hero and deserves the recognition for that. She is a great example of doing the right thing no matter what, and she saw a need and took over the situation. She took something that was awful and turned it around. What she did for me was the best solution at that time. I just hope my life can impact someone the way Mrs. Bise impacted my life. No matter how bad life may seem you need to be strong. These tough situations make us stronger, and prepare us for the future. I often think we sometimes have to go through tough times so we can have a better understanding, so we may help others. I currently have a job that sometimes can be like that bus ride. I know that I do not have to go home with these people and that gets me through it a lot of times. That bus molded me into who I am today, and who I hope I never become.

I often think the reason a person bullies others is because they are lacking something in their own life. Sometimes bulling is a way for the person to deflect attention away from themselves. They think by this deflection that others may not see their own flaws. The person does not realize by bulling others only magnifies that they have a serious issues that need addressing in their own life. Bulling others is not a solution to a person's fears of rejection. By dominating others to the point of humiliation is not a successful outlook on anyone's own personal ambition. No one should set goals in life to demoralize others to the point that sometimes can be to the extreme as death. If that is a personal desire for others to be degraded to this capacity then it is obvious an issue that should be addressed. I think it is imperative that we should seek help for both the victim and the one who is bulling others. I think it is very important to provide counseling for the hopes of discovering the reason these actions were created to begin with. I believe there is a underlying reason for these actions to be acted out. If we do not help everyone then these actions will be carried on. It is time to get a grasp of these unfortunate situations and do what is right. Life has enough challenges to contend with without others contributing their negative action on vulnerable people. We each can make a positive impact on this matter if we all are willing to do what is right.

    I know there are a lot more challenges for kids today than what I had to contend with. I know I use the term kids; however they are young adults in training. We need to train them into a successful person that is able to identify and surpass issues. One obstacle is social media communication. Often times things get misconstrued to the point of destroying friendships or relationships, in a matter of minutes. This is only one example of many trying obstacles our young adults in training contend with daily. Stay in touch with one another in a personal manner is a huge step in overcoming this social communication obstacle. Be strong in every situation for you are *worth every effort in identifying each purpose in becoming a better person.*

I am really proud of both of my daughters. I want to share a remarkable story about my oldest. When she started high school as freshman she noticed there were no anti-bulling organizations for their school. She had done research and wrote up a proposal of creating a support group to be implemented in their school. She identified a need and work very diligently to develop this support group. It was not an easy process she worked on it through the summer while others kids were enjoying their break. She was lining up teachers to help support the group and had a teacher imply she would take it on as an overseer. This teacher withdrew her support once she realized that in fact Lydia was serious. She had made an appointment to meet with the principal still while on summer break. I took her to the appointment to find out the principal was out of town. They told her she would need a county approval. She basically had nothing at this time except her ambition; she had no support from the school or the teachers. This did not stop her for she worked even more diligently to line up a counselor to support her group and now have developed an anti-bulling club. She had many obstacles and was able to surpass them to create something of great value not only for herself to be proud of but a need to many kids. Even if this organization does not excel she has planted a seed that will convey a message and bring awareness to others as a need. It just goes to show when things truly matter, we should be persistent in all efforts to better the lives around us.

My youngest daughter when she was in kindergarten she was elected as the most complimentary in her class. There were awards to each child as a characteristic that they each have. She has always been very complimentary to others. Often we refer to her as the complimentary queen. She is able to brighten many people by identifying their positive attributes they each person possess. Macey has a way to make others feel good about themselves. She has a talent to identify positive things and bring it to a person's awareness to cheer them up. I believe Macey will use this talent through rest of her life as a great attribute to brighten many people's lives around her. I look forward to see what each of my daughters in what they will become. I believe that both have great attributes that will lead them to become successful women one day. We are supposed to be teaching our kids, sometimes I realize they are the ones teaching us.

There are many factors that identify who you are. I have my experiences and self-driven desire to always do my best. To question myself when it does not go so well, what I could do better next time, and learn and grow from each experience and how we react to everyday situations. There are so many ways we can react to life. There can be people who can impact your life in a positive way. Some may even impact your life in a negative way as well. We can grow *from each experience. It is truly up to you, and how you identify who you are.*

Chapter 6: *Remember where you came from and how it has developed who you have become.*

Reflection can be good thing. It gives us a chance to look back where we came from, and hopefully progressed into a better person we are today. There are many things that we can obtain by reflecting back on the past, reflection gives you a chance to think of people you may not have thought about in a while, or a memory of an event that may put a smile on your face, and say I remember when. It gives you a chance to see all the things you have already achieved, and what it has taken to get you where you are at today. Life is filled with so many memories that keep one guessing of what might be around the next corner. Our lives are like a book. There are so many chapters in each of our lives. Sometimes one can hardly wait to see what the next chapters in our life may bring. Life is not always perfect. When we reflect back on memories it can give us strength that we need, to get through what we are currently facing.

  I remember when my grandma had fallen, and broken her hip. My mom had prepared a place for her to stay at our house, so she could take care of her. I loved my grandma so very much. Now she was in a bed and could not be up and about. I would go every evening to show her flowers one vase at a time, and she would comment on how beautiful they were. She even would comment on the silk flowers. She enjoyed seeing them every day, and by me being there I believed helped cheer her up as well. One day I remember the ambulance came to the house, as she was being loaded in she noticed the dogwood blooms, and commented on how beautiful they were. They were the prettiest that year than I ever can recall. After she arrived to hospital she only lasted a couple of days before she passed away. When she passed away they said she had a flower in her hand under her pillow. From that I knew she had been thinking about me at the time of her passing even though I was not there it was like her message for me. For all the times I showed her flowers each night.

  I enjoy gardening now as an adult. I work in my yard a lot to try to make it a place where you can see beautiful plants. My goal has been to have something always in bloom somewhere in the yard. I often think of my grandma with the landscaping constantly changing, and the beautiful flowers that she so dearly enjoyed. I think she would be proud of me if she was still alive. This reflection back brings me great memories of someone I cared so much about, and have incorporated her love of flowers in my own life, as her legacy. I hope when people see my yard they see a beautiful landscaped yard. I see more than just a beautiful yard I see memories of someone who played a major role in my life, and how her legacy still lives on. With each flower, and every year when the dogwood blooms, I cannot help to think about as she asked them to wait before being loaded into the ambulance. Remembering how she noticed the beautiful dogwood blooms. Spring is my favorite time of year for that is when most things bloom.

      I never had known either one of my grandpas. My great uncle seemed to fill that void. My great uncle was into raising cattle. He lived on large piece of property, and enjoyed trading cattle. My dad once had gone to select one of his cows. I wanted the black one, and my dad wanted the red one. I was petting my great uncles cat, and it went running into the fence where my great uncle had placed the cows. The cows were in an inner fence so we could see the ones for sale. The cat had startled the cows, and the red cow that my dad wanted broke through the fence to get away from the cat. My dad then looked at me and said "which cow did you want?" We came home with the black cow. That was the best cow I could do anything with her. She would be lying in the shade, and I could walk right up to pet her. She was more like a dog than a cow. I even could ride on her back like a horse, she did not mind at all.

My great uncle every summer would take my brother and me to the cattle auction. I recall this one time when I wanted to sit on the first row. My uncle said no, that he did not want to sit that close, so we all sat a little further back. That same auction this big bull came in the arena and blew its nose from one end arena to the other side. Everyone that was sitting around the arena had this bulls slime from its nose on them. My uncle leaned down to me, and said "that is why I do not like sitting in those seats." We all had a great laugh out of it.

I would go to walk the pasture with him often. Sometimes I would step in the manure, and he always would tell me there is no need cleaning your shoes until you leave the pasture. I think this can be applied into our daily lives as we go through certain situations. We need not to worry about every detail until we realize what the whole situation may be. I think sometimes we focus on what the problem is more than what can be done about it. Sometimes we need to be patient, and identify what the whole problem is; instead of just one aspect of it. For if we know the whole entirety of the problem, then we have a better understanding of how to address it.

I had attended a mandatory seminar through my job many years ago. I had to listen to a speech that was about how we should not sweat over the small things, and how that everything seems small when we look at it as a whole picture. I believe that this is able to apply to our everyday life. We do have control over our lives, and should make the best with every situation. We should not worry about the things we do not have control over. We should dedicate our efforts to improve on the things that we do have control of. I feel often the life lessons we can learn even from our childhood can be parallel to situations or problems we face today. Reflecting back on these great moments can make us realize that there are people in our lives, who have helped mold us in who we are today. We are able to witness people living their life as a legacy; so that we may have these great experiences to remember them by.

  Reflecting back is a way of bringing back great memories. Memories are things in the past, and as each day passes we are creating new memories, so we should make them great. With every sunrise there is a new beginning to make a lifelong memory for someone to reflect back on. It is up to us to make our own legacies live on.

  Living your life in a manner that is true to yourself should be evident to others. Sometimes other people perceive you differently than your intent. One should reflect on the reason why. One may need to focus on your delivery to others in a more positive manner. Our journey in life is a percentage of who you think you are. The other percentage to our life's journey is who we have become. By reflecting on your life we can see how we influence the people around us. The *people around us are people who care. We should care about how our life impacts their lives. We can make such a positive influence just by our reflection every day. Reflection is a way to evaluate oneself in identifying who you truly are.*

Chapter 7: *Be happy with who you are.*

The two things I hope I will be able to keep my whole entire life, is good health, and happiness. Some people may choose wealth and fame. I do not care about wealth or fame. To me that is all materialistic and leave no personal space and I enjoy my personal time. Many times people measure success by what a person has, and not by who they are. I know we may not have control over our health, other than eating right, and exercising which may not be enough for some people. I do feel we have control over our happiness. By identifying what makes you happy and trying to live a life that engages in the activities that fulfill your needs is where happiness begins. Doing pleasant things for others can bring happiness to you. Being there for a friend can bring happiness. Having a good laugh with family, or friends can eliminate stress that otherwise might be present. Often times in my down time I reflect back on my day. Sometimes I just have to laugh at how I may have conducted myself in a situation, or how it may have transpired. It is good to laugh, even if it is about yourself. We sometimes live in a serious world that can drain the fun out of us. It is good to have a fun time, and share it with others. We should not worry about things, and focus on fulfilling our happiness. Life will swiftly pass you by, whether you are happy or not. I would rather spend my life happy, and hope to spread that happiness to others around me.

    I remember the time when my wife and I had gone to St. Thomas. It was the best trip I have ever experienced. We had so much fun. I still talk about it, and often recall some of the times that we had. We went sailing, snorkeled with sea turtles, and sea trekked. We went to St John one day rented a jeep and drove around the island taking in its beauty. We also went to the British Virgin Islands. We went to Soggy Dollar bar where we had to swim to the island, and everyone's money was wet, and they hang all dollars up to dry. We went to Baths on the British Virgin Islands. We toured St. Thomas observed its beauty as well. This is just a few things. It was an awesome trip. I think that it is important to do things that can give you joy every time you think about it. I can honestly say that week I was so happy. We had planned this trip in great detail and it was jammed packed with activities that we both enjoyed doing. It is great to know that we can do things on a daily routine to have a happy life.

I was watching an interview about Michael Phelps, after his final swim in London Olympic Games of 2012. Michael is the most decorated medal Olympian of current times, and has a total of twenty two medals. Out of the twenty two medals eighteen are gold. This is a major accomplishment. In this interview he discussed his time in London, and how once he got there he was so serious about his swimming. While he was so serious he was not swimming his best. He said once he started to smile, and was happy is when he started to swim better, and started winning more gold medals.

I think happiness is very important in all that we do. Happiness comes from within. When we are happy we are able to be better at what we are doing. In life we can be faced with serious situations, it is important to find happiness in every aspect of our lives. We are a better person when we are happy with whom we are. Identify what makes you the happiest. Once you have identified what makes you the happiest. Try to identify what creates this happiness, and try to apply it into every aspect of your life. We all should be happy with ourselves in every aspect of our life. Happiness is the key of success in identifying who you really are. If at times you do things that make you feel bad it is important to identify these as well, and try to avoid exercising on these behaviors. The path we choose is the path that we tend to continue building on. It is best to build always on happiness than to live a life of regrets. If being around positive people make you happy, then try to surround yourself with people that have that positive impact on you. If you are surrounded by negative people it is essential to be that positive force in their lives. By being that positive influence you can bring yourself happiness. Sometimes we are that positive force that others need. This can be great because, you have a gift to share with others. The gift of happiness that otherwise might be gloomy. I think that people who are in a role that can influence or impact many lives; it is essential to live your life of happiness as example for others to follow.

   Life is often filled with so many questions and expectations of who we really are. It is how we answer each question and accomplish each expectation that affects our happiness. Realizing our life has many avenues or directions to lead us into many experiences that develop us into the person that we are. We should always stay focus on our outlook on life and our own ambition in life. We should ask what we are devoting our efforts for? Are our efforts fulfilling our happiness? Identify the purpose of our goals and are these goals for ourselves? By accomplishing our goals will it give us a sense of achievement for a happier person? One should be able to identify happiness through being thankful and by demonstrating a positive attitude. One should be able to look around and realize quickly how blessed we are. We each have so much to be thankful for. Being *thankful allows us to realize the gifts we have been given in life. Sometimes we are the ones that are to give these gifts to others. Happiness is often balanced by give and take of our gifts that we have accomplished. Thankfulness is the realization that we are blessed and to acknowledge our life as a celebration of positive attitude that leads us to happiness.*

We can either be leaders or followers in our journey in life. I feel we can learn from both paths. Followers observe mistakes or undesirable results of other people's life, and choose not to make the same mistakes in their own life. If a person is the leader they will take ownership of their own journey, and are adventurous at times. They are creating that positive path for others to observe, and take note of their own personal experiences. Taking on the leader role can be rewarding for they can reflect back on all their accomplishments that they have achieved that no one has ever experience before. In the leadership role we can see similar situations and grow from them and we can learn so much from one another's experiences.

Materialistic things are not what identify happiness. I have been asked "are we ever happy with ourselves?" I believe yes we can be happy. I realize sometimes we are in constant search for something better. I believe we should always search for a way to improve on our journey. Through the journey we must seek where our happiness comes from and build on that happiness. I feel everything we do, builds on the next layer; if we are not happy with the first layer then it is evident to identify where our break of happiness began. To find happiness we must be willing to start over with identifying ourselves. We each are experimenting with every effort in life to fulfill our complete happiness. I believe we must be content with our own self. I think if you are not content with yourself then that is where the challenge begins. Doing great things, that is what makes us happy. Try to do a good deed, and then evaluate yourself. See how you feel after completing these tasks. People's amount of income does not buy happiness. Happiness comes from within each of us, and should be explored and experimented with to find that inner happiness. Every person's idea of happiness may vary somewhat from someone else's idea. We so often go about our daily routine, and wish we could make an impact on others. We can, however, we first have to identify our own inner happiness, before we can share it. Some of the happiest people are the ones who give so much of themselves. They may not be wealthy in a materialistic sense, but they are wealthy in their inner happiness, that they give to others each day.

One of my favorite songs is "Boston" by Augustana. I would encourage anyone to listen or purchase this song for it has a great message. I have always liked this song, now that I am writing this book the words mean so much more to me now. In life a lot of times we live our lives from one day to the next. We live it in the same manner, and expect change or a different outcome. To have a change we must be willing to change ourselves. We need to accept change into a life we are intended to be living. Living our life should be a fulfillment of our inner purpose of happiness. Once we find our purpose it is important to conduct in this same positive manner to others. It is not until we exercise these positive changes that we will become happy. Just discovering our inner purpose does not fulfill them. We must be willing to express ourselves in this positive change. Changes occur every day and it is important to control these changes, and drive them in a manner that is for our intent and for our purpose in life. When we are receptive to our own driven purpose, and are willing to act on our good intention, that is when positive change occurs. We are constantly sending out messages. We should always make certain it is our intent of our inner happiness. People will identify you by what they experience. Our moral ethics can impact or influence others around us. If we have good moral ethics then people will notice these characteristics, and expect these patterns. We are driven by our actions, and not just by our intent alone. We may have the best morals and intentions, however, if we never exercise them, then they will never become revealed. Living a life and accomplishing our potential to its fullest, is a life we can be proud of.

    I know sometimes when we get distracted from whom we are meant to be, or our purpose, we should try to start over and focus on the things that truly matter, and what make us happy. Many times people have trouble in identifying in who they are. How should anyone else be able to identify who you are? How can they identify with you if you have not identified yourself? If we find ourselves questioning ourselves on how others do not really know who you are, then we should try to figure out the reason why. It could be a matter of finding your inner happiness, and the willingness of sharing it with anyone around you. Over time we can develop ourselves in a person we can be proud of, or over time we can develop ourselves in someone we do not even recognize any more.

      Have you ever reunited with someone you have not seen for a long while? You realize that you do not even relate to them anymore and you wonder what happened. You may question how did that strange person transformed into the person who they have become. We sometimes are the one that has changed. Change can be good as long as the reason is for our self, and for our inner happiness, for that is what matters. If we do not even recognize ourselves any more then it is time to realize there is hope in becoming that person. You have to set goals of becoming the person of our inner purpose, and realize it takes time to master these goals. First step in any situation is identifying the problem. If we cannot identify what the problem is then how can we address it, and improve on it? If we realize we are not who we wish to be then we need to make that change, to become that great person that makes you happy. We have to be willing to start over if that is what it takes to find who you are, and the happiness that we all seek. We may have several things that may be inspiring to us. It may be a song, a word or phrase that someone said, or a book.

There are many things that may inspire us in becoming that happy content person that so many people seek. What is important is to find the right inspiration to maximize your happiness. Once we find what maximizes our happiness it is essential to live our life so that we are able to convey this happiness to others.

I have had the pleasure to work around a great surgeon recently. I had known him all the way back when he was in his fellowship at my current job. I got to work beside him for three years including fellowship. In those three years we became not just a great surgical team but great friends. I started this saying after each case or when we just went through a challenging time. I would ask him "You Happy?" This became my saying and it just stuck. He would always reply "I am Happy." I would tease him and say if you are not happy then none of us are happy. My point was that we have to be content with every aspect in our lives especially when we are influencing other people's life. Happiness comes from within. When we do a great job it should make us happy. That is what I call taking pride in what you do. I think taking pride in what we do every day is so important. I had taken great pride in helping him each week. He recently moved back to his home town to be closer to his family as well as his wife's family. I miss working with him; however I know he now is truly happy. He is a great surgeon, and he will be a great asset to his new employment. He now will not only be happy professionally, but in his personal life as well and his wife will also be happier. She never settled in, or felt at home in Atlanta. I am proud for both of them, to finally find happiness. They currently have the two young boys, and they give them such great joy in their lives. I think these boys will also be happier being raised closely with their grandparents. I know the grandparents will also be happier as well. By making this move so many people lives will be much happier just by one decision. That just goes to show every day we are faced with so many decisions, and how it can affect other people's happiness. Happiness definitely impacts who you are. He is a great person. He had written the best thank you card, when he was moving away. I was greatly touched by his kindness. He expressed his personal thoughts in a way of only I could hope my life could impact others. It is a great example in how we should let others know what we think about them every day.

Chapter 8: *Inspirational thoughts written by me.*

I wrote these inspirational messages sometime back. I came across them while I was writing this book. I would like to share with you the words that came to me many years ago, and how they have helped me. I felt it seemed appropriate to go in this book. Hope you can see the encouragement in them.

<u>Can you imagine?</u>

Can you imagine if the ocean was dry, and the mountains were flat? We would have so much more land. We on the other hand would not know what the ocean would look like, or the mountains. We would miss the beautiful things that God has created. Have you ever *imagined how many drops of rain or water it would take to fill the ocean? Have you ever imagined why the ocean stops at the shorelines like it does? How many grains of sand it takes to make a beach along our beautiful shores? How mountains stay formed and do not just collapse due to gravity over time?*

I may not know how many drops of water it takes to fill the ocean, or what makes the ocean stop at the shoreline. What keeps the mountains standing tall? Life is filled with mysteries that I may never know the answers to. As I walk the shoreline and feel the gentle breeze. I have the reminder of someone who does. The peace and contentment just hearing the crashing of the waves and feeling the gentle breeze, the soft sand is a reminder of how blessed we are that God created this for us. We could not have these beautiful creations and have a lot more land but I am so thankful we have these reminders of how much God loves us.

The flight of a bird

One day walking along a path I discovered a bird preparing a nest. Day by day I watched this bird placing each twig and gathering the right combination to create this nest. Then the bird laid her eggs in this carefully prepared nest. She sat on her nest day after day occasionally taking a break to get some food for nourishment. Then her patience finally paid off, her two eggs had hatched. They looked so helpless. No feathers and their eyes were not opened. The mother bird did not give up hope. She knew they had to depend on her. The mother bird gathered up food and gave it to her little hatchlings. The helpless young birds began to grow. They fully trusted and depended on their mother to take the proper care of them. The baby bird's eye opened and they were doing so well. They were growing up so quickly. They started growing their flight feathers and the mother taught them to exercise and how to balance. She started testing their ability to fly. One day I walked by to check the birds to find an empty nest. As I looked around I spotted them. The mother was still beside her young to help if any trouble arrived.

As I walked home I started to realize how my life is like the flight of these new birds. See God is always there for me. Before I was even born there were certain preparations that had to be made to make sure I would be in a loving caring home. You know God lets me make my own way sometimes but he is always there if there is any trouble to help me, and to guide me back into the safety of his loving arms.

Time

Days so swiftly come and go, our lives are very similar to that of a day. If we are happy and content with our lives the easier it is for each day to pass us by. If we are miserable our days can seem like an eternity. Time is an interesting concept. We can go through our lives and not realize the importance of each moment we have to spend together with our loved ones.

If we were in the hospital because our premature baby was in intensive care unit not knowing if our child would make it, every passing minute would matter to us. Why it is every minute do not mean as much to us otherwise. If we escaped being in a deadly car crash by a second, that second would make a difference to us. So why is it we go through our lives as if we were promised the next second, or minute, hour, or day? We should cherish our time we have to spend with our family and friends as if it was our last second to spend with them, for we will never know when it might be our last moment with someone.

God's love is always there every moment in time. From the creation to the end of time his love will always be there if you will just let him into your life. Each breath we take our life seems like just a day of peace and contentment. All the heartaches and pain we place there for ourselves. We have a brand new chance every single day to have that sweet peace and contentment into our lives so it is really up to each one of us to make that choice.

These inspirational messages can be just words. I believe if we take the words and ponder on the meaning behind each one then we *can have a more peaceful life that develops into whom we can become. In our hectic world we can all use a little peace and contentment that only God can reveal to each of us.*

Chapter 9: **Good intentions.**

I know we all have heard the saying "The road to Hell is paved with good intentions." I know that is not a pleasant phrase, but to a certain degree I think it is somewhat true. Let me explain, I think good intentions are great, at least you are trying to think good thoughts, and not trying to do bad intentions. When we only use them as thoughts, and do not act on any of them then we are not helping anyone including our self. Whether it is that we run out of time, or we are just too busy. Helping others can be rewarding. If we intend to do such activities then we should at least make an attempt in fulfilling them, no matter what others may think. Set aside time for others, in the end you will be glad you did. Today people do not set aside time for one another. That is the key to getting to know someone is devoting time to them. People are worth the time, for we all want acceptance, and like to feel a part of something. Being a part of something is having a purpose. For some people their purpose is to just be there for others. The more we share our time, the easier it will become. We have made ourselves unavailable to others for too long. Now we have to work at things that we should never have to work on at all. For example being kind to someone, or devoting time to spend with friends, or family. Seems like that there should be no issues with connecting with people whom we care about. Often our hurried world where it seems all that socialization that is so important is falling by the wayside. I just hope we do not lose our caring nature that gives so many people a purpose to carry on. How awful it would be living a non-caring society.

  When I was a young boy, there was a young adult that offered to take me fishing a-lot. To a young boy, like me that was the greatest thing. I used to enjoy fishing. Finally the day came that we were supposed to go fishing. I gathered up all my gear the tackle box, the fishing poles, and dug up a bucket full of worms. I patiently waited, and my friend never showed. I was devastated, I could not understand. Through a child eyes this was a major expectation which was a failure. I suppose this was one of my first times to experience an intention that was not fulfilled into actions. This impacted my young *life of how important that good intentions should be transformed into great actions. To this day when someone doesn't follow through with their plans, it brings back the remembrance of this childhood fishing trip. Now as an adult I do understand, that sometimes we get busy, and have a lot on our minds. We sometimes forget things that we intended to do. This is an example of a great intent, which never came to reality. I think that this past experience has been a life lesson to prepare me of current challenges. I also think these experiences also have made me more cautious of the people I interact with. No one likes feeling rejected. I believe it is fine to have good intentions, as long as we follow through with them and let them become what we do. This experience has made me more aware of what I should do. I try not to make promises. I do not want to set anyone up to feel bad, if something comes up, or I forget. I might say I will try to, or remind me if you do not hear from me.*

There are many reasons why people do not follow through with their intentions. I think it is imperative to always strive to keep our promises to ourselves as well as for anyone else. I think we each have a parallel experience that we can relate to these similar experiences that can mold us into a better person. What one intends to do should extend as actions of their true purpose.

Often managers seem that they have lost their compassion, to the average working employee. They are more interested in numbers and graphs; I realize the importance of the numbers and graphs. We all are more than just a number on a piece of paper. I know we have so much more to each of us, than just a statistics, or just another number, for their graphs. I feel sometimes that is all they see us as, is how we can influence their study, and not who we each are individually. I have seen this behavior time and time again. A new manager comes in, and initially it is a great change and things seem great. Over time they all seem to lose sight of working in the same manner as the rest of the staff. They place themselves more superior to others, and in their minds they are. This to me is very sad to see for they have lost touch with their inner self, and reason to accept a managing position in the first place. I think a major role is to be supportive to the staff as issues arise.

   I recall a time when I witnessed an issue that occurred at work. It takes a certain amount of time to reprocess supplies to be used again. This process cannot be altered and it takes a certain amount of time for it to be done correctly. The managing team questioned why it took longer than what they thought it should have. If the managing team were in touch with reality, they would have known this for themselves, and not had to question it at all. They would be able to foreseen the issue and address it or change the order of type of cases. They could address this issue in many different ways. Instead they made a decision to interrogate the working staff that prepares these items on a daily basis. The lack of support is the issue in this circumstance. They fail to realize that support in this situation would have been more powerful, than any numbers they would want to plug into their graph. They would love to plug in a perfect turn around number, but they fail to realize that reality is reality. It is more powerful to support, than to tear down someone's pride. To them the number is so important; it seems to be more important than treating your own staff with compassion and support. This job is so below them, they never would be doing this hard work themselves. The reality of being supportive and compassionate in their job is a failure. This failure may cost them the best employee and hard workers in the entire department.

Our instrument technician is the best, however, I am afraid due to the lack of support from our managing team, has cost us more than a disappointment this time. The managing team is always telling us to support this person, yet they cannot even live it themselves. I think if you tell someone to practice a certain behavior, then you should live it yourself. This is always so frustrating when people who are supposed to be in a role of managing, and set examples to rest of staff. When I see people in these types of situations it makes me realize how blessed I am. For I know who I am, and not afraid to live it. For knowing who you are, and being truthful to yourself is so important. For if you cannot even identify who you are, then how can you support others.

Unfortunately in managing roles it seems people isolate themselves from others. They lose that personal touch that could make such a positive impact on so many people's lives. I have even noticed at work that all the managers sit together at meetings, at lunch, at any gathering. They have lost the most valuable resource of success which is the personal touch. They have lost the trust and dignity of what it takes to work in unity with others as a team. They have placed themselves in an isolated place of knowing and caring about the average working class in their eyes we are just another statistic and not a person. They often micro-manage meaning they cannot even trust their own managing staff without following up and checking to make certain tasks are being performed by their own managers. They want you to think by checking up on you that they are supporting you. Actually all they are doing is magnifying their distrust they have in their own organization. I feel that I work at a great place and everyone does a great job for everyone takes pride in what they do. Distrust is a way of destroying morale in a workplace. Everyone works efficiently and they do not need the constant micro-managing approach to fulfill their task. These behaviors are just a way of ensuring that the managers have a purpose. They are unable to relate any more in a co-working environment I suppose that is why they cannot interact in a personal level anymore. They think if they are involving them self as a personal level then they would not be respected. I think that is where they are wrong. If managers were more personal and wanted to truly understand their team as individuals; they would become more trusted which leads to respect.

No one wants to be commanded around like we are incompetent. Each day I am so thankful to not be like them, and feel like I am above everyone, and too good to do many tasks that I would require from others, for in reality we all are important.

      I recently attended my nephew's graduation. I like to share one of the speeches spoken to the young graduates. I think it something we each can apply to each of our lives. "There was once a carpenter who was up in his years. He was very talented. He was asked to build this one last house before he retired. He was well known for his quality and skills, he was the best. He had agreed to build this one last house. Day in and day out he would work at building this house. He was worn down and tired. He decided to take short cuts and not use the best material. He seemed to be not concerned of his reputation of great quality and skills that he had earned over previous years. Once he completed this last house the inspector came by to look at the house. The inspector gave him the house to live in for the rest of his days in this house. The inspector had given the house as an appreciation for all his dedication and quality he had developed over the years. While living in this house the carpenter often thought I wished I had known; for I would of use the best material and taken more time to do things differently." We each have things we are building on in life. We may not be a carpenter, but we are building ourselves with each decision. Build each decision and choices as an impact that you can be proud of. Always do your best, for you never know when the choices are for our own foundation of success. Life is better lived with great pride than lived with regrets of what we should have done.

Our life is like a reflection in a mirror. What you put out for yourself will be what you will receive for yourself. Just as we use a mirror to examine our outer appearance, and make adjustments to an acceptable image, it is important to reflect on our inner self, and be willing to improve, and adjust ourselves to allow our inner goals to be reached. Often time people think if I do this no one will ever know. The next time rolls around you think wow nothing bad happen the last time, so what is the big deal. We keep changing our direction of our personal inner purpose. We realize one day the person we once knew is now not the person we even can reflect on, as our true inner self. There are many different directions in our life that can influence our path of our truthful purpose. Just the way mirrors need cleaning on a regular basis so that we can see ourselves clearly, so do our lives. We need to clean up our intentions on a regular basis, and verify that they match our inner goals of our purpose. We should reflect on our own life daily to verify that our path matches the direction that fulfills our inner goals.

The life example we set for others are received by our every action. These actions are what people have to identify who we are, or what kind of person we are. If we have trouble reflecting on our self, just imagine how hard it must be for others to identify who you truly are. We should experience life with great confidence with who we are. It is also a great example for others to identify you by. If we are not happy with the image that we see in our own reflection, then it is time to examine the reason why. Make a mental note to set goals to achieve the person you desire to become. We have to be willing to make a change for ourselves to achieve our inner happiness. We are the one in control of our own expectations, and we should allow ourselves to be proud of all our achievements that we have faced and conquered. Mirrors may reflect our images so we can have a vision of our outer appearance. Happiness and truthfulness is what identifies our inner purpose, and will be what reflects our inner self.

Images are important to us. We are constantly setting goals for ourselves, so we can have that image that others will notice, and want to interact or involve themselves with. The most important fulfillment of our reflection of our self should be for ourselves. We can be our toughest critic, and that is a good thing. We should be constantly challenging ourselves to become a better person, until we become the best of our abilities to match the vision of our purpose. Vision is great for without vision we would be blind, and being blind is not where any of us should set our goals. If we are not able to see or identify our obstacles, and attempt to surpass or overcome them; then we are blind to our inner purpose.

I currently work part time for an eye surgery center. Their slogan or marketing phrase is "a difference you can see." I think that *phrase is so clever. I hope my inner goals matches that phrase, and that my life can be a difference for others to see. I want my life to be that positive force that others can identify with, and it will be able to support my purpose in every aspect of my life. Being able to see yourself in every aspect of life is a great way of identifying your needs, and a way to examine yourselves to become the best at all we do. We should set an example that you will be able to identify that you are able to live your life, and have a vision of a difference you can see.*

Good intentions are not bad if we are willing to follow through with them. Remember intentions are a promise and how important it is to be true to others as well as to our self. It is what you do with each intention we are faced with, and how we conduct them into actions that identifies us as individuals.

Chapter 10: *Your purpose.*

We *each have a purpose for our existence. Some of us think it is only certain areas of our lives that our purpose is required. We are not allowed to pick and choose certain areas of our life and pick the best aspects of our lives, and say that this is who I am. I feel we all have a purpose for all aspects of our lives. We should dedicate our full self to be true to ourselves in our complete life. We should not just say our purpose in our life is just our career, religious, friends, and family. We need to be able to identify our whole inner self. What you are made of, your thoughts and desires or goals. What direction you want to take, each aspect of your life helps in identifying who you are.*

It is so important to always be true to all aspects in your life. We never know when we may be preparing our future, with the experiences we face today. I have been faced with situations in my life that I did not even realize the purpose of them until now. Some situations may even be revealed in the future. It may seem like coincidence that we may experience a situation in the past, and how it has prepared us for the situation on hand. By always being true to yourself, you will be living your own life, and not what you think others may want you to live. By living your life freely then you will recognize the preparation, and know the purpose of a current situation. I have experienced these types of situations in my career. It has seemed that one area has built on one experience, and what I had chosen has led me in the direction I am in today. I often reflect back and realize. If I had not made certain decisions, or if things had not happened the way that they did, I may not be working with and where I am today. I think even in relationships that also apply. If we pretend to be someone that we are not, and we make decisions that build on what others think. We should realize each decision leads to the next. For a happy life it is imperative to always be mindful of how each decision impacts the next, and how we are constantly building our own path. Suppose I had pretended to like my wife, and married her for the wrong reason, I feel my happy married life I experience today would not be as happy, and I would be living a constant regret. So many people get married for the wrong reason. They are seeking a better life. They fail to realize that if we are not who we are intended to be, then we are not living a better life at all. There are many reasons why people get caught up in relationships that are not matched for them. It may be for money, or it may be the person they seek may be attractive, or could be popular, or a famous person. There are so many different reasons why people choose a different path in a relationship. Often times because people choose these paths they later realize the decisions that they have made, have not brought the happiness that they thought that it might would and should have. By knowing yourself and being happy with yourself, the choice you make in choosing the right person is someone that magnifies these feelings. If we stay in tuned to whom we are, and what, or who makes us happy then we know we must be making the right choices. Our sincere happiness is what we all should strive to achieve in all aspects of our life, for that is our purpose. I believe it is not coincidence that this is reality, and that certain paths are prepared for us without our knowledge at times. If I had not been true in all aspects of my life, and pretended to like things or dislike things then that could have led to a whole different path. I would not be as happy with my choices, for I would not have been true to myself, and living an experience that is not who I am. I think this same concept applies to all areas of our lives. It is so important to always be true, and to always be aware of anything that may impact you now or in the future. You are living every moment as your own decisions. That realizing how this all builds one decision to the next, it is constantly building on your purpose in life.

We all have choices, and what we do with the choices not only can impact us today, but also the future. This is why it is so important to own each of your decisions, and to always be true to yourself for it will affect you either now or in the future. Whether you already know who you are, or still trying to figure out what your purpose in life may be. It is great idea to do a self-assessment every day to make sure you are in proper alignment, and that your life matches your inner goals. Sometimes it is so easily to get off track of whom you intend to be. Remember intentions are a promise and how it is so important to be true to you? Intentions are dead not unless you act on them. We all have some better or stronger qualities in our lives and some we will need to work even harder at improve to match our inner goals. We should set our goals to match our lives, thoughts, and not what others think of who we are, or should be. The inner goals should be all about who we want to become.

My daughter just told me about one of her close friend's dad had committed suicide. I feel there is a purpose for me writing this book. I feel if someone can find their inner goals, and see a purpose in their lives, and work on them than there is always hope. Hope is something that we believe in even if we have not ever experience it before. My intention or hope is this book might help someone out, before they feel there is no hope left in their life. No one's life is hopeless. Sometimes we may feel we are in a hopeless situation, but there is always hope for each of us. One is to plan a future that is good and full of hope. We are not to throw away our hopes and dreams, because of a situation looks hopeless. We are to believe in what we hope for. Every life is worth living to its full purpose. Living your life can be challenging at times. We are to look beyond the current trials. Every trial has a victory, sometimes it seems hard to see. It is important to realize that there is a brighter future, and current frustrations are just temporary. We should live each trial as a positive impact we are being molded into a stronger and more knowledgeable person. We should stay focus on our purpose and not be distracted by current difficult times. We all have challenges and some seem impossible to overcome; however, no challenge or situation should take control over your purpose. Is life always perfect? I would have to answer no life is not always perfect. Life I believe should always be worth living for our intended purpose. We should never give up on ourselves keeping a positive perspective on life is a basic step of fulfilling our intended purpose. Sometimes life seems unfair and all odds are against us just keep on searching for the purpose of your existence and focus on your brighter tomorrow. Behind each storm is a sunny day and occasionally even a rainbow. No one should allow themselves to become so vulnerable that they lose sight of themselves. Giving up on who you are and wanting to end one's existence is NOT the answer to any situation. We each are here for a reason or a purpose we should always be willing to explore ourselves in knowing who we are.

Life has many great things to offer each of us; we just need to be patient in receiving them. We each are God's creation, and he has a plan for each one of us. I know I have a lot of work to be the person I need to become. Through daily self-evaluations, I know I can improve on them. Even if it is small improvements, it still is an improvement that is closer to my inner goal. I may not always know what God's purpose is for my life. I cannot even imagine what his plan is as a whole. His thoughts are not mine, for his thought are far more superior than anyone of us are even capable of imagining. I just have to trust that before I leave this walk of life that my purpose will reveal itself to myself, as well as others. For if others can see your purpose you know you have left a legacy behind for them. People will have memories of you. It will either be good memories or they will not want to recall them. Let us all live a life that we can be proud of.

I would like to share a story of when I was a young boy. I decided one day that I was going to run away from home so I packed my suitcase with just my stuffed animals. I got my suitcase packed and was in the process of running away. My brother and sister were up on swing set yelling through the hollow tube. "Mom is coming to get you, better come back." They were trying to warn me that I needed to come back; of course I ignored them and kept going. My mom finally caught up with me and spanked me all the way back home. It was a good thing that my little short legs could run faster than her. As soon as I slowed down there she was with another spanking. I wanted to share this story with you, because sometimes the things we experience as a child can be parallel to experiences we encounter as an adult. One may ask how this story can inspire me in an adult situation. It is through these experiences that we realize there is a message behind each experience. The message I took from this is that in life we are going to be faced with problems, and how that we may not like these problems. We should not run from these problems, we should confront each one. As a child I chose to run away from my problem. I had made a choice to turn my back, and to run as fast as I could from it. In this situation it only made things worse. As an adult I am faced with problems every day. It is important for me to acknowledge these problems, and be willing to address these problems. Another message to take from this is that my brother and sister were up on the swing set and yelling through the hollow tube. They were trying to warn me that my mom was coming, and were trying to encourage me to come back. I think sometimes we have friends or someone placed in our life to give us guidance or advice in our own situation. We should acknowledge these people. Some people may have similar experiences, and can give us guidance or support that we may need to help us with our own problem. The other thing that I took from this experience is what I had packed in my suitcase. I had not packed anything that would have been beneficial for sustaining life; it was what was *important to me. I think it is important for us to identify what is important to us in our life and to strive always to keep them close to you or involved with yourself. I think it is important to acknowledge what is close to you, and to try to keep it a part in our lives through the many changing stages of our life as possible.*

We can learn a lot from our experiences from our childhood. Behind every experience is a message and a story that should be shared. We need to find the meaning behind each experience, and learn how to direct it in the right path for our inner purpose. We all have a certain purpose in our life, and our experiences will mold us and be a building tool to fulfill our purpose.

Sometimes life is like a team. Everyone around us makes up the team. The life team is what we know as our society. We have our own contribution that often impacts others around us. By impacting others, you are making an influence on them. Everyone has their part in life to impact one another. Ask yourself what kind of team player am I? We need to realize that it takes each of us to create such a powerful team. How should we use these powers? Should a person use their powers to build up or tear down? I think we should all evaluate our own life. We should make certain that we are the team players we intend to be. Often times we intend to be someone that we are not. We each have our own game plan. We sometimes just fail in doing our part. Once we have successfully done our part, we can proudly say "I have made a positive difference today." Positive people should be the ones leading the team. Often times it seems the society's team is run in a negative perspective. By living our life in a successful manner of our inner purpose, we can make that difference for someone.

We all are a part of what should be a great team. We should always strive to be winners. By being winner means you have successfully achieved your goals or purpose. The team we live today impacts our future. Our future is being driven by our choices we make today. We should all strive to be the positive all-star players that others will not easily forget. Where is our team spirit? Without the team there is no need for cheering. We must realize we are a part of a life team that identifies us as who we are. Life is not going to cheer you along without your effort or support. We have to earn every cheer. By earning each cheer, one realizes that life does take effort to become successful.

Every successful team has a great strategy plan. What is your strategy based on? Each person has their own plan. We just have to be successful in fulfilling our own purpose in life. Living our life in the realization that we all have our own strategic part in life can be rewarding at times. Keep focus always that each life you encounter may be impacted in the future by the way you live your life today. Positive people should make greater impressions on our society's team. Realizing at times it may take several people focusing on a particular task to successfully complete it. We all have our individual purpose in life. There will be times we will need to unite our thoughts with others to achieve certain goals. We sometimes are in control of the game plan for the team around you. Being responsible for the game plan, we must realize we are impacting a whole team not just ourselves. Taking charge one should realize, you are now a part of a support team as well as a leader. What direction are you going to lead the team? Keep check on the direction of the team to make certain that everything is in proper alignment of goals on hand. Evaluating efforts of a team for a certain task may require support to successfully achieve such goals. Often time's people fail to realize how important support really is. Supporting someone is a powerful attribute to have. Often time's people forget to support others around them. Helping people in any capacity is a form of support. We should never be proud of actions that are degrading to others. We all should remember to strive to be part of a winning team. The team is counting on you to do your part. By doing your part successfully each day helps in identifying who you are, and what your purpose is in life.

Chapter 11: *It is easier being who you are, than to be who other people want or think you should be.*

I find living my life that identifies me in whom I am, can be

challenging enough. Did I make the right decisions today, or what should have I done differently? Did I offend someone, or was I misinterpreted? The only one who really knows every aspect of my life is me. Something's make me so proud of myself. How I may have took charge of a situation or conducted myself in a challenging time. Other times I wish I could have a redo. We all have circumstances that we wished we would have handled differently. It is those times we should reflect and grow. It is ok to tell someone you are sorry, as a matter of fact that does make you a stronger person. It shows that you do care. Caring about others and how you may impact their life is a big step in identifying who you are.

I would like to share a story about the time I baked a cake. There is a lady I worked with who brought into work a wonderful peppermint cake. It was so delicious. I ask for the recipe. I thought it would be great to bake for an upcoming family event. The recipe called for a box of Jiffy cake mix. I accidently used Jiffy corn muffin mix. You can only imagine the texture of this unique cake. It was a little gritty. I took it to my family event anyway. Despite the texture my niece loved it. I simply replied "you know this was my first time baking it, so it may be even better next time." Every time I recall this experience I cannot help but to smile. I often tease about my peppermint corn muffin cake.

In life often I can be just like this cake, if I am not careful to every detail in my life. Things may be different than my initial purpose. I find I must acknowledge my full purpose and apply these new discoveries to my life in a successful manner. Life has many ingredients, for we each are the ingredient. I like to call ingredient to life our behavior. Each behavior is chosen by each individual. Behavior is how we each choose to project our inner self to others. The behavior that is observed by others on a routine basis will be the identification you will earn. These behavioral patterns lead to your personal reputation of who you are as an individual. Everyone's behavioral decisions are required of them daily. People may have bad behavior from time to time, for we all cannot expect our lives to be flawless. Through challenges is when our behavior is put to the test of who we truly are. Just knowing your desires does not fulfill them. Just as a recipe requires certain steps, so does my life. If these steps are altered then the results may not be ideal to anyone's expectation especially my own. I have my own expectation of each situation and I must evaluate the best outcome for each one then apply myself to meet this expectation. I think it is imperative to be true to each detail and to allow each one build a positive person that we each have potential in becoming. Once we have applied the ingredients in the right steps we then will need to mix or blend them to begin a creation of something to be used for intended purpose. In life we must apply our daily behavior into an expectation that surpass our goals of yesterday dreams. We apply ourselves to the lives around us; this is the mixing or blending. This step is what I call sharing we must be willing to share who we are with others. Next is baking the new mixture to become a new transformation to a solid formation. In life we must be able to apply ourselves to others to be a successful support or help to others. By applying yourself and supporting others is a demonstration of a solid and stable behavior. People seek solid interactions from others. We as society do depend on our surroundings to help support our reactions. We need to give others a reason to validate kindness. We finally get to my favorite part of the cake the icing. We apply icing to create a pleasing look and improve the cake's taste. In life we sometimes are only recognized for how people know us. Just as the icing is to improve the cake we are to improve our society with every effort. I think our otter appearance can make an impression to others. We should not decide a person is who they are by appearance alone. Some of the best cakes are the ones that the icing may not be the most attractive. Some of the best people are not always gorgeous people in outer appearance; their true beauty will always shine through every layer. We should be willing to share our whole self in every layer of our life. We can have our cake and eat it too. This means with applying ourselves in every discovery in life we can enjoy and share who we are to everyone around us.

   Con artist has mastered many ways of collecting money from innocent people. Con artist has made it their job to prey on others, who have worked hard to earn their money. One of the ways of preying on people is identity theft. Once a person realizes their identity has been stolen, it is very difficult to reclaim ones identity of who they truly are. It seems all efforts of identification have been jeopardized, as a mutual trust that has taken years to establish through interactions. Identity theft financially can be devastating. Identity theft can be socially as well. Just the way financially identity is stolen, so can ones social identity be altered to become someone that they are not. Sometimes we are our own victim of this identity crisis, by misdirecting ourselves into a person of undesired actions. I have been around people who try to live the life that is out of character for who they truly are. I do not think people just wake up one day, and they are living a strange person life, a person in which they do not even know anymore. I think this happens over a period of time, when people start letting other people influence who they are. It seems easier to just pretend you like certain things. It gets easier next time to be influenced in the other direction. You may think that is who they think that I am, and they may think I am not interesting in whom I truly am. I have been in situations that I was able to identify, that this is not who I am. I have to be true to each situation that each experience matches my purpose of my own identity. I have to take responsibility for each action and direct my life in the direction that best matches my inner goals. Do not be a victim to social identity theft, be aware always of who you are, and direct yourself to maintain your true identity. It takes a bit of work to be yourself at times, but in the end it is easier. By being true to yourself, you will be happier in whom you really are. What makes you happy? What are your hobbies? Do you like watching sports? What is your career and does it influence you in being someone different? Who is your spouse or friends and are you yourself around them? When you are around your family, are you yourself? When you are around people of a religious beliefs or relationships do you act any differently? These are just a few questions, one may ask themselves. You can make your own list, or add to this one to ask yourself. We should be proud of whom we are in all situations, and not in part of them. If we find ourselves not being true to all aspects of our life, it may be time for a change. True friends will accept you for whom you are. If they do not accept you, then they never were your friend to begin with. By being true to yourself, you may realize so many factors you have not even considered in years.

  I do not like when people say they do not care what other people may think. In identifying who you are this is important to have this mentality. Personal ambition is great. That is what one should do in having a successful self-evaluation. When people use this comment they are usually referring to a situation that impacts other people. They are going to do what they want and not care if what they are doing is going to affect another person in a negative way. That is what they really should say. There is a difference in the way we conduct ourselves. If you truly do not care about how we treat one another, then it may be time to do a long look at yourself. It is important to identify why we do not care anymore. Not caring can lead to bigger problems, if you do not believe me then just watch the news one evening or CNN. They are filled with stories that have gone bad. I am a firm believer that it is never too late, and we should never sell ourselves short like that. We can all improve ourselves no matter how too far it may seem. I have heard people say they have done too many bad things and they feel that there is no hope for themselves. Everyone has good qualities in them. Sometimes we have to dig really deep to find it but everyone has some good qualities still in them. We all should be trying to build on the foundation of these good qualities. The turnaround for some will be hard, and may need encouraging along the way. We should never feel that we are too far gone to be a good person. Some people have chosen what may seem to be an easier route. Becoming a better person may take more work initially, but as we start living our lives and change for the better it will get easier. People around you will start noticing a change as well. You may notice that doing good things are very rewarding.

On my current job I work around a nurse who for the longest time had a tough image. She wanted everyone to think she did not really care about anything, an image that is sometimes easy to fall into. I have noticed a change in her. She now is married and has two sons. She has been trying to build on positive actions toward others. At first everyone did not give her a chance. They treated her like the tough person they had known for so long. I have noticed she does not want that image anymore, and she currently is striving to prove she is a good person who truly cares about others. Just the way we wake up one day and realize we are not the person you once were or should be. That happens over time and just like proving to other people you are trying to become a better person takes time as well. As a society sees you over time that is who they think you are. It may take some time for people to see the true you as you make a change. Be patient, do not expect just because you are in process of improving that other people will instantly change with you. Once they notice that you are different for a period of time, and realize that you are striving to connect with who you are; then they will become more accepting of whom you truly are, do not give up if it does not occur as quickly as you like. Therefore I would always encourage people to always be true to who you are. Not to start living in a different style of life, because it is very difficult to make the change, but it will be worth it.

Our life can be like the seasons, and how that it changes over a period of time. When we live each day, the changes are so minor that we hardly even notice. Over a year's time we can see the difference in each season. Through each season we experience storms, and a lot of weather diversities. After these diversities, the weather pattern goes back to the season we, are currently experiencing. Some areas of the world hardly have any changes; they have same type of weather pattern year round. These areas however still experience storms or diversity patterns. I can see similarities in my life that are like the seasons. I go through life living each day as a new beginning. If I only focus on my life as each moment, and do not take a look at it as a whole. I will lose sight of important details of myself. My life is constantly changing, just like the seasons. If I do not keep a close check on myself, then these changes can be so slight that over time these changes can change my inner self and my purpose. Reflecting back and keeping a check where I have already came from, and the challenges I have already achieved. Reflection at times can help me *keep focus on my goals, and to verify that I am on the right track on achieving them. There are going to be storms in my life or diversities that I will have to face. I need to acknowledge these changes, and realize that it does not have to change my inner goals of who I am to become. I believe that through these minor changes in our lives that go undetected over a period of time, people realize one day that they are not the person that they had planned on. We all make bad decisions from time to time and it is okay. We should take these times and acknowledge them. Keep your inner purpose your first priority in becoming successful in who you strive for. The inner happiness that is so important in our life is a good tool to measure our success with. Some people's lives never change through their life. For some this may be good, for others they fail to realize how that their life has impacted others in such a negative way. We all should strive to be that positive force, or that great friend to the lives around us. Just like the weather, we all have a pattern that identifies each of us. What people experience over time is how they respond to you. If your life is a constant storm people will seek refuge or a safe place to be, just like our natural weather patterns. People like consistency in the people that they are involved with. Consistency helps in building structure, and character for each relationship that we encounter. We all go through changes in our life. This is a normal process. It is how we handle these changes that identify us in whom we have become.*

Chapter 12: *Everyone has a story.*

Some people do not have any issues talking; it is more trouble for them to be quiet. I am more on quiet side, so I seem to do more listing than talking. Regardless if you are the one that cannot keep a thought as a thought and have to talk about everything or if you have to be prompted to speak, we all have a story to tell. I am usually quiet at work because there so many people, who will dominate my conversation any way, then take over the whole conversation. What is the use? They do not really want to hear you they want to hear themselves talk. I am sure with me being on the quieter side that many people form an opinion about me. I may not have a lot of words to express my inner self. I believe we all have a story to tell, and that we can learn from each other's experience. I suppose there are many factors why I am a quiet person. I have been through situations that I feel so out of place, because I do not have the gift of gab. Some people have great stories to tell, and tell them well. I get why people may not want to converse with me, for I know I am not as entertaining as most people. I do have great thoughts; I am just not great at expressing them. We all have strong points, and we all have weak ones. This is one of my biggest faults, is conversing with people. I get so frustrated with myself at times, because my weakness hinders me from learning more about others. When I am able to communicate easily with someone it is great. I enjoy being with people that I can communicate easily with. It is like I finally connect with someone. I just wish I could be more like this in all my interactions with people. I think sometimes I am afraid of rejection, but what I fail to realize is that I am already getting rejected by my lack of communication. I am so used to being behind the scenes, that when I talk I feel like I am in the spotlight and that makes me feel uncomfortable. I think that is why I am more comfortable with one on one personal conversation. I like to converse on a more personal level than a generic conversation that normally takes place in a big group of people. I like to listen to someone and to talk in a more significant conversation more on a personal level. By writing about one of my biggest faults, which is communicating to others, is a way of identifying it, and shows that we all have areas that we need to improve on. The way I am treated through my faults and the way that it makes me feel is enough encouragement for me to grow from these experiences. I may not be great at expressing myself to others, however, that does not make me a bad person, even if I am perceived that way. I still have the good morals just not many people will get to know what I am truly made of. I would like to improve on this fault and I am sure if I can be placed in positive situations on a regular basis, I should become more comfortable with it. Communication seems simple, and it is I who needs to overcome my struggles and grow from each situation. I know I can, by having repeated positive interactions will help me build up my confidence. I suppose my feeling of insignificance that I have endured over and over through my career has played a role as well. I find often times people will be willing to tell their stories. They often do not want to hear the stories you have to share. This interaction can make a person feel their stories are insignificant. The people I interact with often tell their stories in great presentation. They can make a story about cleaning grout out of their shower sound adventurous and exciting. I have been out of town and been on vacation and people will not even acknowledge that I even was missing. I need to realize we are all a significant person, and that we all have a story to tell. Our stories are our experiences. We all have many experiences that occur each day, whether someone is willing to listen or not.

I work a second job and often a close friend and I go outside to eat at an area where there are park benches. The setting is very relaxing, but we converse there, and talk about everything, our personal life, work situations, anything it is great. I usually do not open up like I do on these Fridays at lunch time. My friend is a great person, and has helped me through some tough times that I did not even know how the inner part of me would be able to cope with the situation. He would always have words of encouragement. He does not cast judgment on the stories, just listens, and offers advice or tells me a whole different angle that sometimes I may not have even seen. It is great to have a friend who accepts you for who you are. It is beneficial to share our stories, and to grow from them. Sharing my stories has really helped me through some challenging times that only a true friend could help me through. I just hope my friendship has helped him as well. These times we have spent being there for each other has helped me to develop into a stronger person that identifies me into whom I am.

One Friday I went to eat lunch at the park bench setting. My friend that I normally converse with was off this particular Friday. I had tried to plan to eat lunch with someone else and those plans were rejected by the other person. I had a challenging week and so I really wanted to talk to someone. I decided to go eat alone and just enjoy the outdoors. Once I arrived there was a young man sitting at one of the benches. I proceeded to sit near him on a different bench. We *started talking to each other. It was very easy talking to him. One of the first things I noticed is when I spoke he would listen. I am not use to having people willing to listen. People are often times distracted or interested in telling their own stories. He was a very motivated young man, who was full of ambition. He had a desire to help others. I was greatly impressed of his desire. He had expressed to me how he had done some bad things in his life. I tried to encourage him by saying we all have done things that we are not happy with in our lives. It is important to identify where we need improvement and move forward. I also told him that he seemed to be heading in the right direction for having a desire to reach out to help others. This is a great desire. Through conversing with him I felt I was able to encourage him. I learned so much from him. He asked if I was familiar with the term "spoken word" I replied I am not familiar with that. He asked me if he could share something with me, I replied sure. He had shared with me how he was interested in the arts and hopes to be a motivator speaker then to break out in "spoken word" (which is similar to rap only more artistically done and often is a storytelling or poetry.) Through "spoken word" he tells me the title was sole like what is on your shoe. This message was telling me his story of his experience. His method made you listen to his story. I never experienced anything like this in person before I was intrigued. Through listening I learned about his experience in prison and things he had to endure. I learned in prison he had a desire for religious beliefs but had to reframe for the other* prisoners seek any form of weakness to prey on. I learned about his plea to the judge to be set free. Things I never even have had to experience or even spoken to anyone that has gone through these trying times of being incarcerated. There were so many experiences in this little message that made me realize the gift we all take for granted which is our freedom each day. I continue to encourage him I told him he had a special talent. I said often times when people speak they lot of times are just heard; with his talent you cannot help but to listen. He shared with me he had been in prison in four different states. I had a sense of calmness and not being afraid of him even though there was no one around. Through conversation I learned he had just got a job and was to start the very next day. He told me his job was going to pay minimum wage. I shared with him my own story as when I completed my surgical technician program how I had to take a job as an orderly. I worked in that role for nine months before I was able to get a job as a surgical technician. I told him he was blessed to have a job. There are many people in this area that are not even able to get a job. I told him that he at least is moving forward in the right direction. I really enjoyed talking and hopefully encouraging this young man. This young man was encouraging to me as well. He helped me realize we each should appreciate the things we have, especially our freedom. I also realized I have a gift of encouragement to others. This gift can become a gift for me as well. I realized through this experience that a purpose in my life is to try and encourage others. I have written many things of encouragement. It is not until I had the opportunity to exercise this gift, that my strength in encouraging people around me was a realization of a direct impact on them. This conversation was my way of realizing that I can be there for others even when I have no understanding of their experiences. As he walked away he told me that it was nice talking with you. I told him good luck. I believe I made a difference in a life that day, it was a great day. It was a great experience to try and encourage someone from a dark past to keep trying. I feel I was placed there for this young man for encouragement. You just never know when you can help someone. I have heard a saying "you never know when you are in the presence of an angel." One may say that this individual was no angel, for me he was, for he made me realize one of my purposes in life is to encourage people and the importance of exercising my gifts. This individual was as much sent for me as I was for him. I wish the best of luck to anyone who is starting over with another chance in life. We each have a story that can encourage others; it only can encourage them if you are willing to share it.

I recall one of my stories I have not shared with many people. It was when I rode in back seat of a police car. We were in the process of building our home. A police officer had come by while I was cleaning up some of the construction. He had asked if we had seen a little boy that lived up the street. He was missing. After the officer left I decided to go to search on the property next door. This property is a *large tract of land at least eighty acres, and on this acreage is a pond. I was concerned that this small boy would have wondered on that property and fell in the pond. I knew I had to search this property, and so I crossed the fence and started searching for the young boy. I found him by a stream that was overflow for the pond. He was playing and his dog had not left his side. I spoke to him and picked him up, and found the search party. They had officers on horseback searching as well as people on foot. They took him back to his house, and so the police officer offered to give me a ride back home. I rode in the back of a police car. It feels great to be able to find a missing child, and it is not in a tragic manner which very well could have been the case. Sometimes in life we are like this boy. We set out with a purpose, and let things distract us. Next thing we are in a strange environment, and nothing is what our initial intent was. It is important to try to stay focus on our surroundings always, and the people that are in them. Be willing to share, and listen to each person's story.*

    Everyone's story is worth listening to. We all have experiences whether it is a childhood story, or more current one. We can learn from one another experiences, and become a stronger person in return. Sometimes it is not what we do for ourselves it is what we do for others that make a difference. I have shared many stories in this book that many people have not ever heard before and have a different angle of my experiences that people may not even realize that side of me. I believe we should share our stories and let everyone know who we are.

Chapter: 13: **Only you are in control in identifying who you are.**

We are faced with so many decisions every single day. These decisions impact us in whom we are. We go through life every single day, and our lives are filled with choices, and decisions we have to make. Some decisions are easy and some will require much thought. How we experience these situations help determine who we are, and identify each of us individually. It is important to acknowledge our decisions, and how it can impact others. Through our decisions, and choices we are developing our character of individuality. These characteristics set us apart from the rest of our society. We are the one who is in control of our own personal lives.

We should live our life in such a way; it can set positive examples for people around us. We are constantly being watched or judged by others around us. In identifying ourselves it is important to know always we are the one who is in charge of our own lives. So many times you may hear "they made me do it, or it is not my fault." We should not place blame on other people regarding our own personal lives. We are directing our own paths through our journey in life. We are to take responsibility for our self. We are the ones directing our intent into actions of a purpose in fulfilling who we are. We are the one making our own decision or choices. Some choices will be good, and some may not be so good. In the end we are the one making these decisions. So many times people's intent is to be good, however, they let society influence their decisions, and let them make an impact on their lives. We should be the ones making an impact on other people's life for the better. By living a life that is pleasing within ourselves we can make that positive impact. We should have a positive attitude about everything. Sometimes life is filled with so many difficult challenges, that we may never understand. I believe we go through certain circumstances to make us stronger. So we might have a better understanding of a situation of our own life, or for someone else. We may be able to help someone else with a similar situation, because we now have a better understanding through our own personal experiences. I believe we all have a purpose and we need to be able to identify our purpose, and to live it the best you can. There may be many factors that may hinder us; however, it is important to acknowledge the obstacles and to overcome them; so we can become the best person that we possibly can.

      Some of our challenges can be degrading or can be demoralizing. No matter what the situation may be always be true to yourself. We can learn from our challenges. From time to time we may be down on our self, what I call a pity party. Do not let the pity party rule who you are. I think sometimes we go through these times so we can reflect on certain situations. We should not dwell on it but reflection can be a benefit. It gives you a chance to evaluate the situation. A chance to say "I did not like the way that happened, and to make a change for the better next time." It is in these times we should identify why we feel this way, and to address the circumstance that makes you feel this way. It is great time to set goals, and to achieve each of those goals. In our lives we should not be constantly down on ourselves. We should live our lives with excitement, as every aspect of our life is a new adventure. Every single day that we wake up it is a new adventure, and we should make the best of it. Our time is all about how we can do things better and more efficiently. We live in a rush up world so it is important to take time for you. You should always be proud of whom you are, for that is what identifies you. Do not be afraid to show people who you are, and that you are proud of all your achievements. By showing people who you are can make you stronger, and people around you will also become stronger as well.

You will be able to do things that you never thought were possible by being the positive person that you are. Take control of your own life, and live your own life. You are the only one that can control every aspect of your own life through each decision. It is time for us to take control of our lives and live it to its fullest.

Have you ever been around someone who enjoys pointing out all the things you have not been successful in by their perspective on life? These same individuals like to tell you how they would handle it, as if their way is the only logical way. I really do not need my faults to be a constant reminder of failure by their perspective on life. I realize I make mistakes and come short to other people's expectations. I try to live my life to match my own goals, not to live my life to match society's goals of success. Encouraging is more powerful than discouraging someone. Encouraging is a form of support. Persuading people to become to their standards of an ideal lifestyle and not allowing a person to use their own judgment is an unacceptable standard. People should be free and live their life the way they are intended to be. Controlling a person's thoughts to the point of changing a person's direction is not beneficial at all. Just because someone has experience does not make them an expert. I do respect other people's level of experience on life's many challenges. People should respect that there may be a different approach to each situation and that these approaches may vary from individual to individual. I think the best approach is to have an open mind that *each person has their own way of addressing each issue. Just because someone approaches an issue differently does not make that individual stupid or wrong, they just have a different style of handling their issues. We each can do our part in supporting each other with an open mind. We may even learn from their style of handling issues. I find identifying who you are is a privilege of freedom one possesses of projecting your inner-self to an outlook for others. Everyone has their own identity that magnifies their unique driven purpose. Each person is different just like a fingerprint we each have our own mark on life. Each individual purpose translates to a lifestyle of its own ambitions of goals and accomplishments. Life is challenging enough without living to a lifestyle that surpasses approval of everyone's expectations. A person will not be able to please everyone and should realize the person that needs to be pleased is themselves. There will always be different standards of expectations from society it is your personal standards that should be first. Often time people tell others what to do without even realizing or considering the direction or the intended purpose of the individual. By interjecting themselves in every detail and telling someone how and what they should be doing is not helpful, it actually can be harmful. No one likes to be controlled like a puppet. Sometimes the hardest part is realizing the strings are no longer attached for both the controller and the one that often times is controlled. It is time to free ourselves from these strings of bondage and discover our own mistakes and our own success of who we are.*

I often discuss how you are to take control of your own life. This same philosophy also applies for others we are not to take control of someone else and control their identity. Often people try to fix other people instead of providing support. One may have good intentions of helping, some people's intentions however is to change or fix a person into someone that they are not. A person should be identified by their own expectations and actions, and not to just meet our terms of expectations. We as a friend or support need to allow each person a chance to express themselves as characteristics of their own lifestyle. We can advise or support others but not direct them to change who they are intended to be. Each person is in charge of their own destiny in life. Controlling a person's decisions is not allowing them to explore and find the person that identifies them as an individual. A person needs to be able to persevere over their own challenges to become strong in themselves. We can be more helpful by supporting than by trying to change someone who is content with who they are. This approach of changing someone will only change the way they feel about you. Change must be desired within a person and exercised on a personal level of each person's individual goal. We must let a person decide for themselves of what direction their life decisions will lead them. This can be challenging to allow this freedom of someone we care about. I am not insinuating that we should never be there for others, for support is so important. We can share our life decisions and how they have impacted us through our journey in life. We can express certain goals of achievement. We can be supportive many ways. The truth is my life is a mysterious daily challenge that I am constantly trying to improve on my own purpose. I am not worthy to dictate to others of how they are to live their life; when my life stands in need of great improvement. If I am always directing other people's lives then I am not focusing on my own direction in life which can lead to my own failure. For I know I am the only one in control of who I am. We should allow people we care about to discover that they as well are the only one who truly knows whom they are.

There are many things that identify us individually. How we decide to live each experience, and allow it to mold us in whom we are is what makes us all unique. I recently went on vacation and noticed in many gift shops that my daughters enjoy going into, there was a shirt that seems to catch my eye. It had "YOLO" written on it. YOLO stands for "you only live once." I thought what a great message. Probably some people would look at that as a given permission to party and to party more. My perception is we only have a one shot of knowing, and living our life to our fullest personal purpose. We each can have good qualities. Some people may feel rejected or unappreciated to the point of giving up, or being a failure in their personal inner happiness. It is important to realize we only have a one shot of being successful or truthful to ourselves. We should not let experiences or the way we have been treated affect us in a negative manner. My message is that you only live once so it is pertinent to make the best out of every aspect of your life. If you have always wanted to skydive then skydive. If you want to be that difference in someone else's life, then make that positive difference. I know someone who skydived at the age of eighty. She is a remarkable person who seems to live a life with no regrets.

    We each have individual decisions or experiences that are different from each person. These experiences are similar enough that allows us to have things in common with people around us. Relationships are created from the support that either you give or receive. Even if it seems that there is nothing in common with someone, there seems to always be a parallel experience that we can share with someone. By showing support you are showing that you think of them. Many times we are not supportive for a numerous different reasons. Often we feel we have not been asked, and we do not want to intrude. We may think we are not experiencing the exact same situation, or perhaps we may think that we do not have anything in common with that person. Through just living our lives, every day routine can be enough to have in common with people around us. We impact people daily either positively or negatively, and how people perceive us is our legacy that they will remember. Identifying who you are can seem complex or it can be easily achieved. By being true to yourself and living a life that you are to always be proud of. By molding yourself into that inner person that has guided you through your life. Living a life for the purpose we all have individually to fulfill, should be each of our first priority. We know the areas that need improving on and should set realistic goals for ourselves to achieve them. Stay focus of your inner purpose, and let that be the driving force in each decision or choice that we may encounter. Strive to do good for doing good deeds make us feel great of whom we truly are.

Life has many challenges that direct us forward in the path that we have chosen. If we feel we have made poor decisions or choices there is always hope in becoming more experienced in life's journey. Realizing we need to make a change is the first step to that inner happiness that we all strive for. Situations are there for us to grow and learn from them even if we do not realize it at the time. We are in control of our behavior and how we conduct ourselves in our life's journey.

Some people are placed in certain circumstances these circumstances can make a huge impact on others. How they choose to fulfill them can be encouraging, and some a huge disappointment. We all make mistakes, and that is fine as long as we realize them, and improve on them. Your ambition should be to become a better person for you as well as for others. There is nothing wrong with making a mistake. What is wrong is repeatedly to make the same ones, and are not willing to change or realize that there is even an issue. We all live in a very challenging world that has many expectations of how we *should conduct ourselves; it is our inner self that should be our guide. We are to choose our path, and not let society take control over our whole being, or purpose for our existence. Happiness should be the core of our desires, for when we do great things this should be our guide to a successful driven purpose. Success is achieving goals we have prepared for ourselves. Failure is when we are defeated by challenges that we encounter, and do not attempt or set goals to overcome them. We are in a decision to decision type of environment that each one builds on the next. We should focus on the choices on hand to achieve the happy successful person that we all strive to become. We are who we are today by living a life of a free conscience, of doing the best we can at everything we set out to do.*

Recently I heard someone ask a question that has stayed with me. I would like to share it with you. If you were given a short period of time to live, and knew that you only had a day or so to live, would you live your life any differently? This person point was he felt we would try to make things right with people, and live a life with no regrets. I often wonder what hinders us from living this lifestyle every day. What prevents us from constantly living our lives in this manner? We are faced with so many opportunities to fulfill this need every single day. I know at times my priorities are not in proper alignment to successfully achieve these goals. It is through dedication to others, and striving to make a positive difference that one is able to accomplish these tasks successfully. We are challenged every day with our behavior. How we are to conduct ourselves in a productive successful manner is what may influence other people around us. If we did live each day with the mentality that it is our last chance to make a difference, I think every day would be a more significant experience. I feel I would focus more on the things that truly matter, and not focus on the mindless distractions that we encounter daily. I think often times these distractions interfere with my intentions. These same distractions often take me down a path that I am not proud of, or a legacy I would not want others to remember me by.

Often people seek distractions to keep their mind off a difficult time of their current situation. The distraction may be one's work or something else. Challenges can be difficult to contend with when things do not go the way of our intended purpose. There are times we are faced with great sorrow that are difficult. Embrace every challenge as a building experience even if it may be difficult to understand. A building experience is identifying a need of a situation and applying oneself into a knowledgeable positive outcome. I think sometimes distractions can be good as long as they are temporarily relieving your painful experience. I do not feel these distractions should be a permanent identification of who you are. I do feel with time we do have to contend with these difficult times. We should find our inner desires to guide us back to our intended purpose in life. We should not let these challenging times overtake who we intend to be. People handle issues in their own time and some at a different pace than others.

There are different stages in any healing process. Healing is an essential process; for without healing one is not successfully contending with themselves. We sometimes have no understanding of how we are to successfully make it through these trials or frustrations. We are to trust in our strength of our inner self to surpass all challenges. Through our healing process we will become a stronger person once we have faced our challenges successfully. Always be true to you and your intended purpose in all stages in your life. Life can be a battlefield for we are to fight for our own purpose in life. We each are worth the fight. Every experience in life has a learning opportunity to build a more knowledgeable person of whom you are to become.

I work with some extraordinary amazing people. Life challenges can be difficult to contend with at times. I remember two instances that were very challenging. It was through the distractions of work that helped them through these times. One of the nurses I work with was diagnosed with breast cancer. She went through the recommended treatment. This nurse chose to work through her treatments as much as possible. The work distracted her from worrying about her condition and the path of treatment ahead. She did great. I was very proud of her, and how her courage was conveyed to others. Another nurse had her husband who had passed away. This nurse as well worked through her time of sorrow. She as well used her job as a distraction for her difficult time. Life sometimes can be challenging or difficult we are to find courage, to be our strength, and keep our purpose alive.

    I feel every morning we wake up it is the only one of its kind, for we have never experienced this day before, and when the day ends we will never see it again. Each day is unique in that it is time set aside for us, to determine the paths we have chosen, and are the paths chosen the ones we can be proud of, and be remembered by? We impact people every day, and some of our experiences may never have an opportunity to repeat. We should be always mindful of our diligent efforts, and determination of making each day a remembrance that will be worth our time. We should have the recognition of values of each day. How it can make a difference that can be seen, and respected. Even by our best efforts some people may never respect you for your efforts. I think we should be the ones to direct our own paths in a way that will be pleasing to ourselves in achieving the inner goals that we have set aside for ourselves. For if we can meet our own expectations by the actions or the behaviors we express on a daily routine, we should feel content on knowing we have done our best at every situation that each day offers us to overcome.

    Expectations are a form of an idea of how we think a situation should happen. We may not always have control of how others perceive the expectations of the services that we offer. Through living a life that is parallel to our word or promise is how people will confide in you. If we do not live a life that is truthful, or is too busy to complete task on a daily basis, then people may not relate to you. We are always sending a message to the people around you. The expectation of people is that we are to always be true to our word, and willing to act on these promises. Meeting our own goals of expectation that we have prepared for ourselves, is a start of a promise to ourselves. We are becoming the individuals that have full control of our life.

      Disappointments occur when we do not meet or surpassed our goals or expectations. It seems that sometimes we live our life full of disappointments. Overcoming disappointments starts with you. When things go differently than initially anticipated it sometimes is easier to point fingers at others. There is one thing to remember when you point your finger at others there are three more fingers pointing back at you. We are to take responsibility for our own actions. Even through our greatest disappointment there is a positive message if we only seek it. It is normal to be disappointed at times. We should identify our intentions and allow them to set standards or goals for us in the future. Our intentions should be driven by our inner desires and followed through with our actions. We will be able to match our thoughts with our actions to complete our purpose in life. Life is filled with complicated obstacles that one must endure daily. One must be willing to challenge themselves through these obstacles and surpass these challenges. Only you are in control of identifying who you are. Keep focus of who you have become, and whom you are to be in the future. We are always forming expectations for ourselves, as well as others. We are in control of ourselves, but sometimes the expectations we have for other people can be a disappointment. We have no control of how other people conduct themselves.

We may think we may have full understanding of situation, that we may not know it in its entirety. Sometimes that may be why someone may not react the way we think they should. We often think by doing things to our own expectations are equivalent to other people's standards. We may get frustrated when we realize we did not fulfill the challenge on hand. There are many reasons for our frustrations. We may not been clear or on same page as the person, so therefore we did not complete the task to their approval. This is where communication is crucial. There are many reasons why we set certain expectations on other people as well. We expect a certain character or person through our everyday experiences that we may encounter from them individually. I think not only do we use these standards to identify others, but we are also identified by our paths, or experiences that we share with others. Through these experiences is where we develop these relationships that are to identify who we are, and what kind of person we are. We all have a certain expectation for different individuals. It is how a person conducts themselves, or their behavior that we encounter on numerous occasions. This is what separates our *degree of expectations of each person. If we have a poor interaction with a person, then our expectation of that person will be lower, than someone who is inner driven to fulfill their purpose in life. People that fulfill our expectations will be the people we will continue to interact with and want to be around. We are comfortable with people that meet and or exceed our expectation on a regular basis. We set high standards for ourselves so we too may be whom other people will want to be around. The clothes or outer appearance is not who a person is, they are who they are by their inner purpose in life that creates us individually.*

Chapter 14: *Who are you?*

I thought I would close my remarks about this book with the title.

Who are you? It seems to be an easy question, or is it? There are many things that identify each of us. We each have many attributes that transform us into who we are. We have many challenges in life to contend with. It is how we handle each decision that impacts us differently into a personal identification that separates us apart individually. We each have our own personal contributions to society. These contributions are our gifts to one another. We each have a unique gift that should be shared to amplify our purpose. I hope through my experiences that are shared throughout this book of who we are, make us each strive to be a true person to ourselves. No matter what experiences you have encountered in your life it is important how you handle each one. We can each be a positive force in people's lives around us.

Once we have identified who we are, we should ask ourselves another question. This question is "what do I stand for?" To know who you are is a huge accomplishment. This huge accomplishment unfortunately is not the end. We must know what we stand for. Examine your actions to make certain that what we stand for speaks to others as a positive influence. Have I left a legacy for others to remember me by? Will I be proud of what they recall? We each have a unique purpose in life. One should be willing to stand up for the things that they believe in. I think it is very important to believe in yourself. The definition for believe by (Wolfram Alpha) is "to accept as true; take to be true; and to be confident about something." I think by believing in yourself you will be true to yourself and be confident in yourself, which will equal to trust from others. People place trust in many things. The definition of trust by (Wolfram Alfa) is "certainty based on past experiences; complete confidence in a person or a plan; the trait of believing in the honesty and reliability of others." One thing people do not put enough trust into is themself. If we trust our self we will be able to believe in our self. Trusting and believing in yourself is what I call having self-confidence. Living a life that is true to our self will also lead to trust from others. Trust in relationships is developed by honesty and certainty of past experiences. If someone trusts in you they confide in you. I have found for myself trust has to *be earned over a period of time. For some people trust is there from the beginning of their relationship until there is a reason for the trust to be broken. Trust is something that should be respected. Trust is a special gift, that often times I only share with only a few people. When you trust someone you are demonstrating the complete confidence you have in someone. Trusting someone is allowing yourself to become vulnerable to gossip, if you place your trust in the wrong person. I know once my trust has been broken it is very difficult for someone to earn it back. This is why it is imperative to honor a person in great respect so your respect and trust may be mutual. It is through our interactions that we have experienced in the past that will help us determine when trust is applicable. I feel one must trust before they can believe. Trust is formed from previous experiences whereas belief is applying this trust into experiences of a future expectation. Trusting and believing in yourself will help to verify the question what do I stand for? We should live our life to its fullest potential and be proud of every accomplished goal. We should be a strong person to be able to stand for ourselves in a successful driven purpose. By being stronger you will be able to achieve things you never thought were possible.*

I would have never seen myself writing a book. By exploring, trusting, and believing in myself, is how this book is even possible. It all started with when I first met people the next question is what do you do for a living? Who would have thought that would inspire me to explore my inner self, and share with everyone some of my thoughts. We are not what we do, but we are who we become through our experiences of knowing our purpose and developing our experiences into who we are.

Our stories will be what are carried on as our legend. People will recall interactions they have had with you. What I stand for is not always what I would wish to leave as my legacy. This is where our inner self needs to be in proper alignment with what others experience on a routine basis. Through consistent positive interactions is how I am able to develop into what I stand for.

The title of the book WHO ARE YOU was addressed to myself originally. I have discovered by looking at these three words Who Are You I found a brand new word by using the first letter from each word in the tittle. The word is WAY; I realize the "WAY" I live my life is the "WAY" I will be identified as who I am. Seems often in life the answers to our own questions are always there, we just need to seek the answers. Often times the answers in life are even found in the question itself. This book seems to make a complete circle in identifying myself even by the title. I know in my journey I have to make my own "WAY" in life, to successfully master who I am intended to become. Through writing this book I have identified and learned many things about myself. The basic details of this book are not foreign. It is a review of how I should treat others with respect and fulfill my inner purpose in life. This book has many of my experiences *that are important in identifying who I am. I use my own experiences and my concepts to shed light on how it affects me. I often think unconsciously I make decisions in life. It is not until I identify and bring them to light that I can acknowledge them. I have to be able to recognize and understand each issue and take a conscious step to alter them. I must make what was once an unconscious decision and make it a conscious action of a better life to live. By conscious choosing a better way I am addressing myself in a respectful behavior, to let others know that I truly care. Through exploring myself and identifying areas of improvement is how I become a stronger person. I know by just exploring myself is not enough. I must be willing to live my life, and its new discoveries with an open mind. If I never apply these new discoveries to the way I live then it will not be beneficial to anyone. I have a strong desire to make a positive difference in people's lives around me. I am aware that people around me have to be receptive to fulfill these personal desires. I feel if I can influence one person in a day in a positive manner, then I have had a great day. I enjoy helping people; it is a part of who I am.*

I know my life is not perfect. I am constantly striving to improve on myself. I need to be familiar with who I am and what do I stand for, to become a stronger person in whom I can believe in, and others can trust. I am not insinuating that my life is better. I believe that I face similar challenges that other people contend with every day. I have made many errors in these challenges. I would hope through reading some of my experiences others may reflect on them, and realize we each have our own part in life that may be shared to grow from one another's experiences. Even if one reads my experiences and indicates there is a better way of handling a challenge, one still can grow through me sharing my stories. We should compile our thoughts to conclude a plan of actions so we can surpass our current expectations in the future. By compiling our thoughts and creating a strategy plan we are developing into who you are, and knowing what you stand for; this is the beginning steps in believing in yourself.

We have to pursue our desires to become successful in every aspect of our life. I think by pursuing your dreams we are to believe in ourselves. By accomplishing our dreams it gives us great pride in knowing every effort does and will matter. This accomplishment is what is known as success. Success is an awesome feeling. We are experiencing a change that is able to impact others in a more meaningful way. We need to all strive to become champions of our dreams. Dreams are visions of what we wish to accomplish. Believing in yourself is a great start in fulfilling each dream successfully.
I think it is important to believe in yourself when identifying who you are. Sometimes in life it seems to be more difficult to identify ourselves than at other times. Our experiences we face from day to day are identifying us on continuous basis. I think it is up to each of

us to make our own successful path in becoming the person we have set goals on. I think it is so important to identify yourself, before you can relate to other's identity. I feel "you" in the title can also refer to others around you. By identifying who other people are, means you have taken the time to learn who they truly are. So many times we interact with other people the way that they interact with us. Often times this is only one aspect of our life, and so therefore we only respond back in the same manner.

In this book I often express how, I wish people would learn more than just one aspect of my life. This works in both ways. I can see where I can learn to expand on myself as well. I may need to apply this process of expanding my horizons; even if the other person typically only involves themselves in one area. This does not mean that I have to live my life in that same little box. By learning more about other people's more intricate parts of their lives, I can put the pieces together. I can learn more about who they truly are as a whole, and not just in one or two aspects of their lives. It is so important to learn about other people. By learning more about others can strengthen us as individuals, and make us happier with ourselves.

I realize now that I am not the only person that needs to identify every situation as a molding experience, of who we are to become. Everyone has to identify for themselves who they are. By reflection on oneself we realize what it has taken us to get where we are today. It is through our experiences and how we react to them that transport us down the path of knowing that happy inner person. By positive interaction on a regular basis propels us to become a stronger person in every aspect of our life, it also helps us identify our purpose.

I just hope through me sharing myself, it can be a encouragement to someone else, in identifying themselves, in becoming who they truly are. I realize that it does matter that we should always strive for that inner happiness. Through happiness you will find what is important to you. Happiness will be your guide in success in identifying who you truly are and what you are made of. Once you have identified who you are it is important to always remember who you are. Try to live a life that meets your purpose. We should always be proud of whom we have become.

There are so many things that identify who we are. We should accept all aspects of our lives and incorporate them in who we have become. We should be proud of all aspects of our life. Always be yourself. It is easier being who you should be than whom people think you should be.

It is time we make ourselves available to others. We should not class or categorize people around us, as if they were a materialistic item. Everyone deserves the respect of humanity. We should invest our time that we have devoted to learn someone, to praise them as a unique individual. To praise someone is to express something good about that person. Everyone has a talent that they give to society as their gift. We all are people that have good intentions, but let us act on these intentions, and show people what we are made of.

My life is filled with many people that are very magnificent. Through me writing this book I have explored and examined many of my thoughts and philosophy's. I have realized that even the way I have always lived my life and my interactions I have chosen need a great deal of work. I will share with you one of my most difficult challenges. I have discovered this all from exploring and asking myself why. I have struggled with having friends. The few friends I do have I deeply cherish. I want my life to have a more meaningful purpose to others. I have many people in my life who I feel have impacted my life positively, they have a great purpose and meaning to me. I consider these positive people a friend. I desire a mutual friendship where the person I acknowledge as a positive person would like to be more involved with me. I find in life we want to be around people who we feel good about being around. I desire to have that same positive impact of my life for others. I feel if I could impact people positively they would like being around me, they would realize that they are in presence of a friend. I have always presented myself friendly to others and this has always made me wonder why. Why I cannot seem to have a close friendship. I have presented myself friendly yet no one cares to become a close friend with me. I even have wondered what is wrong with me.

Recently through exploring I discovered there is what I call two types of friendships. The first I will call visual friendship the second I will call non-visual friendship. Usually in this comparison one would probably choose visual just by the choices available. Before one chooses they should listen to description of each comparison. A visual friendship is someone who is your friend only when they see you, this is a more superficial relationship. A visual friend is often thought as someone who is just nice. There are a lot of nice people. Often time these people are only acquaintances instead of a friend. A non-visual friend will make an attempt to interact with you even when you are not present. This is a more sincere friendship. A non-visual friend will use all their resources to reach out instead of what they just visually see.

Being a visual friend is very easy. The reason I know it is easy is that I have discovered in my life I have been a visual friend to others. You are able to enjoy others but only while you are present. I realize now to develop a more sincere friendship I must attempt to pursue a more meaningful friendship other than just being nice to others only while around them. I have tested my new philosophy and have realized people often are content in just being a visual friend. I also have discovered that it may take time to develop a more meaningful friendship. I know it is through exposure of my changes that others will eventually acknowledge my sincerity.

I have explored the idea of extending my friendship with other people who classify themselves on a different level by society's standards. I was in great hopes to write about how some of my philosophies were incorrect. I wanted to write about how others can perceive you as a friend no matter what level of society's image is. I am going to share my experience in exploring a friendship of a more superior level by society's standards. I will let each person decide for themselves how this experiment went. A few questions that I had asked myself in this experiment were. Do people respect me for who I am? Does society even give me a chance in knowing who I am as an individual? Is our society content with just having the visual friend mentality? Is our society changing before our eyes without us even noticing? Are we becoming more and more impersonal? How do I benefit from each discovery in becoming the person I intend to be? How do I apply myself in each action or reaction that others project? I feel no matter what happens in life it is important to stand for a representation of who I am in every level of my life. We each have a unique purpose and goals that one should never let others influence you away from your intended purpose. What experience are we leaving to others as our identity of who we truly are?

I have discovered even after I have lived every experience as an identity of who I am, that some people will never take the time to acknowledge you as the person you are. These people use their own ideas to create you as someone you have no intentions of being. This is their perspective of who they have formed as an identity of who you are. Even at times when I have believed that I have been successful in living my life as a testament of who I am, I realize that my intentions are misconstrued into a totally different direction than that of who I am.

I have always attempted to present myself as a reputable person in all areas of my life. My reputation is important to me. I am always building on myself to be respected and trusted by others. I realize that I cannot be respected and trusted by everyone that I interact with. Some people will never see who I am for they have not achieved their own true identity for themselves. I realize now some people will never allow themselves to be sincere even to themselves. Some people do not know what it is to live a sincere and meaningful life. They have been treated a certain way in their life and that is who they have become. They have allowed these actions that they receive by others to mold them into someone else instead of living their life as their own identity. They have failed at what is most important in understanding what identifies them of their own true identity and purpose. Often people allow society to set standards, for they have not achieved sincere standards for their own purpose.

I have shared my experiences and detail through the process of writing this book only with a few individuals. I have worked around these individuals for many years and have shared a whole different angle of myself with them through my writing. I thought my life had been valued in each one of these individuals as a friend. I trusted and respected each one the way I would any friend. I have lived my life to what I thought would be trusted and respected in the same manner by each of these individuals. I realized that some of these were never my friend to begin with. Some have lived their life to receive the service I provide as a surgical technician. I value friendship probably more than anyone else that I know. Having friends is very important to me.

      I reached out to an individual to develop a better friendship with this person. I was exploring with the non-visual friendship philosophy. This individual is perceived to be on a different level by society's standards. This person is perceived as a very selfish individual. In the past all my interactions as a friend were all one sided. I was the one who would initiate any type of interaction outside of work. I once again initiated a conversation to try and expand a friendship with this person. This individual turned my words into a total different direction than what I intended. This person implied that I was trying to expand to be something that I was not. I was only trying to improve a friendship, instead it was destroyed. I realize now this individual was never a friend to begin with. I worked with this individual for well over a decade. Through this whole time this individual never once learned who I was. If this person had taken time to learn who I am then they would have never turned my words to mean something that it did not. This individual felt I was disturbing and inappropriate. The only thing that was disturbing and *inappropriate was this person; to change a person's intent to mean something that it did not mean, to such a degree of not wanting any type of interaction. This person demonstrated a very malicious behavior. I suppose this person has their own insecurities that need to be addressed.*

I know now I should have realized over the years that this person was never a friend to me in the first place. I have always looked over this person's flaws and chose to see only good qualities in this person. I should have seen this person's true identity years ago. This individual use to ask me question like how I was doing, I would attempt to reply then this person would put their hand in my face and tell me "I cannot talk to you right now I am busy." (This is just one of many flaws I would over look.) I am somewhat relieved about the whole experience. This individual did for me what I could not see, which is their true identity of who this person really is. I now can see this person in a whole different light and the insecurities that this person has. I know that all of my efforts of being myself with this individual will be forever lost.

I accept now that maybe, I could have use a different approach to my words. I however, would have never imagined that these words would have ever been received the way they were. I realize I cannot take the intent they were received and turn them into a positive outlook by this person. I will forever be remembered by this individual as what they perceived, and not what my purpose was. This person has mandated that I will not attempt to communicate to them at any level. I am not sure if I would ever care to communicate to someone of this mentality anyways, for blowing things way out of proportion and creating such false allegations. To imply certain behaviors of my intent is wrong, especially when one is not even giving an opportunity to try and clear the misunderstanding up. I would have preferred to make peace with someone than to eliminate all possibilities of resolving a misunderstanding. This experience brings the realization that there are selfish conniving individuals in all walks of life wanting to destroy a person's identity. No friend would treat another friend to the severity that I was treated in this experience. The one thing that troubles me about this experience is the communication shutdown, and to indicate that there was no mistake in their judgment. They persuaded themselves that there was no possibility that they were incorrect. To demand no type of communication identifies that this person has many insecurities that are magnified; as the weak person that they are.

I went to work and met with the operating room charge nurse to request that my assignments to be permanently adjusted to eliminate interactions of any level with this individual. I wanted to comply with the mandated request from this individual. I discovered that this person already validated the same request to the director of the surgery center. I remember what my charge nurse told me she said "Tim I want you to know everyone here cares about you" what a powerful person she is to help strengthen me through this challenging time. She did not even know the details of the circumstances that caused this decision, and she chose to support me. She has taken time to know who I am and the reputation that I live. She also knew how I was the only person who enjoyed working with this person. We always worked well, as a great team. Through this entire experience I have always known who I am and what my intent of trying to improve a friendship; that obviously never was a friend to begin with. It is experiences like these that build character into a stronger person. I plan to learn from this experience and expand my intended purpose to the people who are truly worthy of my friendship.

Sometimes when a person is challenged they react before they take a moment to try and understand the situation. I am sure we all have reacted before we should have. In these circumstances it is important to allow our values guide us to do what is right. By allowing our values to guide us into what is right, we are allowing our morals to consciously direct us into a better person. Often this direction leads us to the realization we are wrong and how we must apologize for our actions. In some individuals they never will admit that they have perceived things incorrectly. In their eyes they make no mistakes or have any types of misunderstandings. They perceive themselves perfect. They fail to take ownership of what could be their own successful destination. It is sharing with others that bring our own intended purpose to reality of who we are.

Sometimes our reality of someone's purpose may be for the good as well as the bad. I have discovered in identifying others we must examine a person for who they are and not who we want them to be. This truthful examination can prevent a huge disappointment in the future. If we allow honesty to be our guide it can lead us to where a friendship begins. It is important to build on something solid not on something you hope is solid. I have acknowledged that in life I have to identify my intentions into actions. Sometimes my intended purpose will still become blinded by others around me. These people go through life blinded by their own insecurities that prevent them seeing anyone as their true identity of who they are. We should never let these blind people lead us into believing our intent or purpose in life should be lived by their standards. We should attempt to become our own individual to whoever can see us for our true identity and purpose.

When I experience poor behavior from others; the only thing I wish is that they would take ownership and acknowledge that they may have been wrong or that they perceived things in a whole different light. Only thing that could be better than acknowledgement is that they ask for forgiveness. For asking for forgiveness lets others know that a person still has morals and that they truly care about others. I know in this circumstance I will never expect any type of acknowledgement much less an apology. I know this because I now can see this person for who they truly are.

I have learned some valuable lessons from this experience. One is when a friendship is one sided and it is you that are doing all the initiation, then probably they are not a friend at all. When someone believes they are more superior over you then they are not accepting you for who you are, then they probably are not a friend. If they have not learned you for who you are then they probably are not a friend. Be aware of who you respect, trust, and confide in. If you have to work at creating a friendship that the other person has no intentions of, then they probably are not a friend. Always be yourself they will either like you for who you are or they will not. Be careful with who you trust as a friend. I realize the best friendships seem to occur without a lot of effort. I also discovered friends are who you confide in challenging times. People that evaluate their life as a different level often think you are after something more, they often think materialistic values and not on a personal level. If they are on a personal level they are into their own vanity. Some people the way they treat others on a routine basis makes me question if they even have a conscience or good morals, or do they just choose to behave poorly? I know not everyone from different economical levels by society standards have this mentality. I believe there are still good people in all walks of life. I have also learned that I have to evaluate people's characteristics as a whole, to know who they are and not only identify the good qualities. I cannot make someone be a friend when they do not have the same desire.

Often people disguise themselves. Best analogy I have is as if they are a wolf wearing sheep clothing. They blend in with everyone outwardly but inside they are just waiting to destroy a person and their identity. This is why it is so important to always know who you are. It is important to live who you are every day. We never know when we might be the next targeted victim of their inconsiderate actions. These individuals are usually selfish and only concerned with themselves and how the rest of the world is at their mercy. By allowing their actions to rule you only fulfill their actions. We each have our own values in identifying our thoughts into a positive action. We each have a meaningful purpose in life. We each should live every day as an example or testament of who we are. There will always be wolves among the sheep waiting to prey on the weak. This should give each of us ambition to always be strong. We can defeat any challenge through strength in knowing who you are.

I shared this difficult experience with a great friend of mine. I explained how my intentions were misconstrued to a whole different level. I also told him what this person implied. After his initial shock, he started talking to me and helping me through this mental challenge. This friend is great at giving me encouragement, or advice, even a different outlook of many of my experiences. This friend knows both of our characteristics as individuals. He was telling me how that I am always looking for the good in others and how this other person creates an anxiety attack on his own employees when they have to work with him. He indicated we are on two different scales of our personal values. I expressed how that this experience made me wonder who else thought these same thoughts about me. He told me it is the individual person who has a problem not you. I am not the one broken. He told me about when he was young he went to live with his grandmother for a while. He was the only black kid at his school. This really bothered him he wanted to fit in. He would talk to his grandmother and she would tell him there is nothing wrong with you. She would say you are made perfect and how that you do not have to change a thing to fit in with others. He also told me we as a society now have a new prejudice. It is no longer black and white. He said it is rich and poor. There will soon be no middleclass. You will either be rich or you will be poor. His next question was where did I want to be? Rich and be superficial not developing a true friendship; or poor and be happy with the people around you. I suppose that could be a tough question for some. I strive to have friends and happiness. For me this is a goal of mine to always surround myself with people who truly care. I find that it is not the amount of money a person makes, it is what a person is willing to share that make them wealthy. I am glad I have control of who I am. I know my intent and purpose in life and it feels great being the person I strive to be as a success in knowing what truly matters. It is important even in the hardest and most difficult challenges to be proud of who you are.

By now I am sure everyone has developed their own opinion on how my expansion of non-visual friendship went. I will now share my thoughts with everyone regarding this friendship exploration. Through my exploration of attempting to develop a better friendship with this person who is perceived on a different level by society's standards. I realized through this attempt the way things transpired confirmed my philosophy throughout the book. There is a certain level created by society that may influence some people's decisions of their level of interactions on a personal level. This individual chose to exercises his intentions as a malicious act against me, as well as many other people as a routine lifestyle. The person in this example I discovered has great issues that need addressing. This person has good qualities; unfortunately this person chooses to allow the bad ones to overrule this person's behavior toward others. This person is very successful professionally and is viewed by high standards by many people. People often only see this person as a successful professional and treat this person by highest standards and respect; respect that this person has not earned on a personal level. It is this person's personal status that needs great improvement to become successful in their own true identity. I may not be respected by high standards professionally by many people. I do attempt to live a meaningful life that whoever can see my identity can respect me for who I am. I must admit my level of disappointment in this example led me to become comfortably numb. Comfortably numb meant I was content of having no feeling or emotions. I had never been treated this poorly before; it was on a whole different magnitude. I was betrayed by someone who I thought was a friend. I never had anyone to mandate all interactions to be withdrawn and report same request to my wife and my job. I realize now by reporting to my wife and my place of employment could have cost me more than the value of this friendship. If my wife and my job did not know who I am they each could have mandated no further interactions with me the same way this person did. They fortunately know me and respect me for the way I have always lived my life. By being truthful to my purpose in life it has revealed the person that I am. Only people who want to see my purpose in life will be able to see who I am. This individual reacted very irrational and responded very inappropriate in their actions. I could not imagine any rational person responding in such a manner. This whole experience was disturbing to me. I could not understand someone who I thought I knew for over a decade would be so unpredictable. I could not imagine the life I live could be translated to receive such a response from anyone. To be treated by someone you respected, trusted, and confided in of such manner is inconceivable. I sometimes now have trust issues with other people I interact with on a daily routine. I have developed some new boundaries and I am very cautious of who I trust and interact with. Being treated in this manner at this severity I realized I was becoming not sincere with any interactions at any level. I would just go through my days without a *driven purpose. I suppose by being comfortably numb was a way of protecting myself. I know I should not let one person influence my purpose. I was shocked initially by this person's actions and trying to make sense out this person's foolish perception. Someone that demonstrates these types of behaviors on others has obviously lost their purpose in life. I do not believe anyone's purpose should be so inconsiderate to others. People that have a meaningful purpose in life do not treat others the way this person treats people. This person treats others as if other people are servants, for this is the only value he has on another person's life. As long as you are willing to do the things that he request then all is good, the moment that things are viewed differently all communication is shut down, for you are a worthless to him. I speak through my own experiences and things that I have observed over the years. This individual does not want to learn who a person is because it requires a personal commitment of personal information as an identity. I suppose that is why he responded the way he did when I was trying to expand and improve on a friendship. He knew this one area he was weak in, which is being personal to others. He is unable to identify his own true personal purpose, much less expand on someone else. Professionally he was finished with me and there was no reason for my existence anymore. I was simply a nuisance to him at this point. I served as no true value to him now. I had done my job as a surgical technician and helped him establish a successful surgery center and helped with staff to best assist him. Every one of his staff had the same story about how he would mistreat them. They do not enjoy working with him. I would encourage each by telling my own experiences of being mistreated initially and gave them encouragement that it would get better. I was the go to person for I knew his surgical routine better than anyone else. When people would ask him what he needed for a case he would have them to ask me. I was always willing to help. He is very good at what he does, he sometimes lacks in detail of things needed. He just knew whatever he needed that I would have it there for him. He did not have to worry about the details for I had already done that for him. I had made certain that everything was in place for a type of surgery that he had not done at his surgery center yet. Once I told him everything looked good, I found it ironic that shortly after that is when I was no longer needed and treated very poorly. It was my turn to be disposed of and treated by his personal standards, which is to be treated like trash. I too was disposed of. It is interesting to see how some people use other people to better themselves, and then dispose of your interactions once you are no longer needed. I still work at both surgery centers but in both all interactions from this individual is permanently eliminated. I am respected at both surgery centers for the person I am and not who I pretend to be. This person often pretends to be nice and is not successful in his efforts. These efforts are received and dealt with in the same manner that he is, not genuine or sincere. He receives the attention he wants through a professional* status. The professional status gives him the respect as something meaningful to himself that is lacking in his personal life. It is ashamed that these actions are just through pure obligations and not genuine or sincere. I have witnessed how he has his assistant go and fetch coffee for him. He is treated as something grand. I suppose once he is finished with this assistant she too will be discarded just like everyone else. He has gone through so many assistants through my years of knowing him. I find people of this mentality are pathetic they are blinded by what they think is their own greatness. They cannot see anything as a respectful and meaningful life. They have chosen society's image and not a true identity of who they are. This is the type of mentality I have spoken throughout this book as the mentality of our society as a whole. People are often viewed as their profession and not the person that lives inside each of us, that identifies each as individuals. Our behavior should always be sincere to our intended purpose in life. Many people have lost their true meaning in life. I often think that majority of our society is comfortably numb today. They are just going through the motions without a purpose. Someone that is comfortably numb cannot and will not understand a sincere and meaningful life. Through myself-evaluation and support from my family and friends I made a change. I have no desire to waste my purpose in life. I do not want to be forever comfortably numb. I want to live a sincere and meaningful purpose in all level of my life. We are to learn through each experience to build a stronger person who does *make a difference in lives around us. There may unfortunately be people just waiting to bring you down. Do not allow these unfortunate people rule your goals and desires. You should always live a sincere life with a meaningful purpose.*

There are many types of relationships that we encounter every day. With every relationship there is always room for improvement. When someone uses the term relationship people often think intimate relationships. This is just one type of many relations we encounter. Relationship just means there is a connection or agreement between two individuals or parties. This connection could be a business relation or any other agreement. Often relationships are formed over a period of time. During this period of time a person evaluates the circumstances and responds to these patterns observed. People monitor the patterns of particular behaviors by the other person. To form any type of relationship it requires a certain amount of trust and respect. Once a relationship is formed we have developed an agreement of respect and trust. Once this trust and respect has become jeopardized this is where betrayal begins. We live in society today where it seems we have many stories of where relationships have been altered due to betrayal. We each have a choice in life. We are the ones that direct the way we live it. Do we live a meaningful life with a driven purpose? Do we choose to support others and develop strong relations with them? Do we know who we are and allow ourselves to become support for others who may be in need? We have a choice each day to either be someone that has a meaningful purpose or we can betray everyone by not living a true life that reveals our full potential of our driven purpose. By living a life that does not reveal your purpose, the person who suffers the most is yourself. By living a life that reveals your identity allows everyone who will, benefit in knowing who you are.

I recall when my girls were little kids playing on the playground they would make new friends instantly. They did not have the same ideas we have as adults they just wanted to play. They did not judge a person for which pre-k they attended, where they lived, what type of cars their parents drove. They had no discrimination of race, appearances, sexual thoughts, or if they were from a wealthy family, or a poor one. They just simply wanted to play. Sometimes in life I think there are so many obstacles that interfere with the way we treat others. I often think if we could be more like these kids on the playground and eliminate our discriminating thoughts and actions then this world would be a much better place to live.

I shared details of this book with an acquaintance of mine. By now through sharing myself with everyone, one is able to realize that typically I am shy and usually I keep my thought my thoughts. He had responded to me by saying that I am an admirable man with many interesting layers and surprises. I find this very interesting for this is the last thing I would ever think of hearing from him. I always thought that my stories would not be that significant to him. This just proves when we are willing to share ourselves is when our purpose can become evident to others. I think by setting one's own life for an example to share by our friends; we all can become an admirable person that has many interesting layers. Even you may be surprised of who you really are. By sharing our life experiences it exposes the different layers or aspects of our life. This gives us a chance to share more than the one or two areas that they typically would experience.

We all have many layers and the willingness to share ourselves in our entirety is a successful beginning. Many people only want to try to know the one aspect that they already interact with. A true friend will embrace every layer as a new adventure, and will accept the complete you. We will have many acquaintances in a lifetime, and only a few true friends who will accept you in every layer of your life. Regardless of discovering the layers alone or sharing them with a friend, each layer should always be admirable, and you should always be proud of whom you are in every layer. Keep your head held high, and embrace the person you have become in every layer. Be willing to share yourself with others. We all have that great inner person that should be set free. Share our stories with anyone that is willing to listen. We never know when we may positively impact a person by our everyday experiences. It is always important to realize our purpose and to be willing to ask ourselves **"WHO ARE YOU?"**

Special thanks:

I like to thank God for all he has done for me and my family. I know there are many challenges in life, and I am thankful to have a God to see me through each one. I know each experiences builds on the many layers of my life. We all have a purpose and a meaning for our existence. I am so glad that God is capable to help me through these journeys even if I cannot even see a way. God is so awesome God that words can never tell the magnitude of his forgiveness. I know I do many things that are not by his desires and he blesses me unconditionally every day. I thank God for allowing me the courage to write this book and share with whoever will read my story. I feel that God should always be our first priority in guidance of our purpose in life.

I would like to thank so many people for their support. I have included some of my friends through this process. My family has been a great support for me as well. I frequently have gotten tested with my patience on the work of this book. Cindy, Lydia, and Macey have had the biggest challenges of living with me through this whole process. My family has always encouraged my inner driven purpose to become successful in every layer of my life.

My parents deserve a special recognition for without the raising that I had received, I may not be the man I am today. My parents taught me the good moral values that guide me through each decision. They supported me through the many challenging trials in my childhood.

I would like to mention a special thanks to a great friend, Terry Williams. I have bounced ideas and shared a lot of this book with him through conversation. He has been very encouraging to me, not just while writing this book but through my life's journey. He often is able to give me a whole new perspective of my own life that often I am not even able to identify that different angle on my own life. He is an amazing friend.

A special thanks for everyone who already taken the first step in making this world we live in a better place. Thanks to all your dedication in your inner self for that is where our happiness, and purpose comes from is within, and not our outwardly appearance. I may not be able to thank everyone individually for the impact you leave as your legacy. I would like to thank each of you for the way you have directed your life in such a successful manner in finding what truly matters, and living it to your fullest ability. There are so many people that have been a successful person in my journey in identifying themselves of who they really are. I have become a better person for the lessons I have learned through their experiences. We all can learn from one another to become a stronger person in our inner purpose *that makes us each as individuals. Everyone's story has a positive meaning behind it. Sometimes we need to realize the meaning that we need to take from each experience. Give thanks to the people around us that make our life a positive influence so special. Thanks to anyone willing to expand on themselves, and their inner happiness, for you make this a better world to live in. Thanks for the willingness to discover what it truly means to be true to yourself, and not afraid to ask WHO ARE YOU?*

WHO ARE

YOU?

www.ingramcontent.com/pod-product-compliance
Lightning Source LLC
Chambersburg PA
CBHW031443040426
42444CB00007B/946